GETTING STARTED IN WOODWORKING™

Furniture You Can Build

Projects That
Hone Your Skills

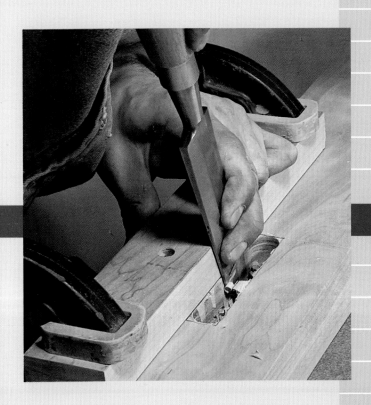

Joe Hurst-Wajszczuk

Photographs by Del Brown

The Taunton Press

The Taunton Press
Inspiration for hands-on living®

The Taunton Press, Inc., 63 South Main Street, PO Box 5506, Newtown, CT 06470-550
e-mail: tp@taunton.com

Editor: Matthew Teague
Interior design and Layout: Barbara Balch
Illustrator: Chuck Lockhart
Photographer: Del Brown

Library of Congress Cataloging-in-Publication Data

Hurst-Wajszczuk, Joe.
  Furniture you can build / Joe Hurst-Wajszczuk.
    p. cm. -- (Taunton's getting started in woodworking)
  ISBN-13: 978-1-56158-796-4
  ISBN-10: 1-56158-796-6
  1. Furniture making. I. Title. II. Series.
  TT194.H87 2006
  684.1'04--dc22

                    2005025600

Printed in the United States of America
10 9 8 7 6 5 4 3 2 1

The following manufacturers/names appearing in *Furniture You Can Build* are trademarks:
Band-Aid®, Krazy Glue®, Masonite®, Watco®

ABOUT YOUR SAFETY
Working with wood is inherently dangerous. Using hand or power tools improperly or
ignoring safety practices can lead to permanent injury or even death. Don't try to perform
operations you learn about here (or elsewhere) unless you're certain they are safe for you.
If something about an operation doesn't feel right, don't do it. Look for another way.
We want you to enjoy the craft, so please keep safety foremost in your mind whenever
you're in the shop.

Acknowledgments

This project would never have left my garage without the assistance of many talented people. First, a hearty thank you to executive editor Helen Albert, project editor Julie Hamilton, and editorial assistant Jenny Peters for their initial guidance and patience as I struggled with the first book to carry my name on the spine.

You'll never know where my words stop and his begin, but my editor, Matthew Teague, has touched every page of text. This book wouldn't have made sense without his careful eye and experienced hand.

I am equally indebted to Del Brown for his thoughtful photography. After all, what's a woodworking book without photos to steer it?

I would also like to thank my former colleague, Paul Anthony. Paul's direction and advice about the nuts and bolts of book writing prevented me from making more than a few wrong turns.

Special thanks to Chad Corley at Porter Cable/Delta, John Otto at Jet, Wally Wilson at Lee Valley, Jason Felder at Bosch Power Tools, Grace DiNapoli at Classic Designs by Matthew Burak, and Lisa Agostoni at Freud Tools. These folks were always quick to loan out tools and provide assistance along the way.

Words aren't nearly enough, but my sincerest thanks is a start to my wife, Kristine. Without her support, patience, and encouragement, I would have never attempted to start this project. I certainly wouldn't have found the strength to complete it.

Contents

Introduction

Having written and edited hundreds of pages of workshop and home improvement material, I've been fortunate to have met and worked with real woodworkers: people who could dovetail a drawer (by hand) in five minutes, plane wispy shavings off the gnarliest wood—one guy could even identify wood by taste. If these folks were to cut themselves (mind you, it would never happen in the shop), you'd discover that sap, not blood, flows through their veins. I'll be the first to admit that I'm not one of them...yet.

If they're what you'd consider woodworkers, then I'm just a guy who enjoys making things from wood. My shop is far from dreamy; you can't tell by the photos, but I'm sharing space with a car, lawnmower, and miscellaneous garden equipment. My home is becoming filled with some nice pieces, but I'm certainly not at the point where I'm ready to quit my day job. Woodworking is a passion, not *the* passion, of my life. And for now, I'm happy to keep it that way.

With that difference in mind, I've geared this book for real people: readers who enjoy making sawdust but still want (or need) time to mow the lawn, go to their kid's soccer game, or paint the house. To them, the "dream shop" is still a dream. Woodworking involves a combination of compromises: lusting for the best tools but not wanting a second mortgage; trying to design a comfortable shop but needing to work around a car or washer and dryer; wanting to improve hand-tool and machine skills, but not willing to embark on a seven-year apprenticeship.

This book is designed to help you enjoy your time in the shop. As you work through these pages, you'll learn how to work with and build on the skills and tools you already have. And when the sawdust settles, you should also have a few attractive pieces to add to your home or give to friends. My hope is that someone may look at one of your projects and say, "Wow, you made this yourself?"

My mentors might flip through these pages, but I must point out that this book isn't for them; rather, it's for the other 99 percent of the woodworking world. If this book gives you the confidence to teach another up-and-coming sawdust maker, then at that point we'll both be real woodworkers.

How to Use This Book

If you've done some woodworking, built (or even repaired) a backyard deck, or completed miscellaneous projects around the house, then you probably have the necessary skills—and most of the required tools—to tackle the projects in this book. That said, it wouldn't hurt to pick up some additional information. Though this book stands by itself, it's designed to complement the first three books in the "Getting Started" series. In them, the basics (i.e., sharpening, routing) are covered in greater detail. You'll also find additional projects for your home and shop.

As in the earlier books, "Skill Builder," "Work Smart," and "Jig" boxes provide useful information to help you move successfully from one step to the next. Even if you're not interested in a particular project, read these sections. Many of the jigs introduced in earlier chapters are used later on in the book. You may also discover a jig or technique that can help (or inspire) you with projects outside of those on these pages.

Whenever possible, I've included "Design Options," offering ways to adapt a project to fit your particular needs. Woodworking needn't be a paint-by-numbers affair. Feel free to experiment with different woods and finishes. For example, if you make the blanket box from cherry or oak, you may choose to mix up a batch of the wiping varnish formula used for the desk organizer instead of hiding gorgeous wood under a coat of milk paint. Similarly, you can build the bookcase or desk from poplar or pine to save money and brush on your favorite color of paint. The dimensions of the sofa table, bookcase, and bed can be easily altered to fit a particular niche in your home. That's what building custom furniture is all about.

Perhaps the best-kept secret to shop success is thinking through a project before you cut the first board. Reading the directions is like building the piece in your mind. Taking time to understand the building process in your head will result in fewer goofs in the shop. You'll still make mistakes (we all do), but that's part of the learning process.

The second secret is not to spend too much time flipping through books like this. These pages won't make complete sense until you've added a healthy sprinkling of sawdust. Now let's get started.

On a clear day you can see the floor. Even small shops can turn out big projects. Only 120 sq. ft. was enough space to build the projects in this book—sometimes two at a time. A big advantage of portable tools is that they can be wheeled around to make the best use of available space.

Tools

Almost every woodworking book begins with a "Tools" chapter. Too often, it focuses more on wants than needs. Its pages might help fill a book, but by discouraging readers from climbing out of their chairs and into their shops, the chapter fails at what it was designed to do.

Having helped several friends build shops from scratch, I appreciate the tough decisions and financial pain that come with setting up. With them (and you) in mind, I've reduced my list of essential tools to a "starter set" and have designed the projects in this book accordingly. You'll have decades to build your dream shop; until then, this list should get the job done.

The first book in this series covered must-have tools. I've added a few more that you may choose to add to your collection. Don't let this list scare you; you needn't buy everything at once. In fact, it's better to start learning the basics before making big purchases; that way your decisions will hinge more upon what feels and works right for you and less upon someone else's opinion.

Just as the quantity of needed tools might discourage beginners from making sawdust, quality is another potential deterrent. "Buy the best you can afford" is a handy axiom, but I've met more than a few woodworkers who have invested every penny into a few hand-forged chisels or a professional-grade über-machine and are then too broke to buy the tools or materials needed to build a birdhouse. Moderately priced tools can do great things in capable hands, especially if you've taken the time to set and sharpen them so that they can perform at their very best. And as the many benchtop tools used in this book demonstrate, bigger isn't necessarily better.

Tools for Woodworking

Woodworking relies on such a cooperative exchange between so many tools and machines, it seems almost unfair to segregate them into distinct categories, but you need to start somewhere. I've divided the tools into "tailless" hand tools and "tailed" power tools, which include both handheld and benchtop models. As you skim each section, pay attention to the "Add" tools. These tools aren't required to complete the projects in this book, but they can make certain steps easier, or at least more enjoyable.

Hand Tools

Hand tools offer the ability to adjust the fit of a joint or produce a finished surface quickly and precisely without drowning out your favorite radio station. You'll also appreciate the tactile feedback hand tools provide. Realize that this isn't a plea to return to some golden age of woodworking. Tablesaws, jointers, planers, sanders, and other "tailed apprentices" make short work of big chores, which can make woodworking a hobby instead of hard work.

Marking and measuring tools

You'll need a few tools to relay measurements from this book, or your head, to the wood. To start, you'll need a good-quality 12" combination square and a tape measure or folding rule. For angles, it helps to have a bevel gauge, plastic protractor, and framing square. To accurately transfer those measurements, you'll need a marking knife (a utility knife will do) or a fine-tipped pencil (I use inexpensive 5 mm mechanical pencils). Sometimes, as when finding the midpoint of a board or laying out a tenon, numbers get in the way. Here, you'll want to use a marking gauge.

Add: Large drafting triangles are cheaper than machine-setting jigs and as accurate as you may ever need. Chalklines are equally useful for marking plywood or establishing level lines when hanging a wall full of cabinets.

Measuring and marking tools. Your basic measuring gear should include a combination square, tape measure, and sliding bevel. You'll soon find need for a framing square, plastic triangle, and protractor. Use a marking gauge, mechanical pencil, or knife to transfer dimensions to the wood.

Handplanes

A sharp, well-set plane can cure a lot of ills. Before I got bitten by the plane-collecting bug, I worked with only a one-handed block plane and a larger #5 jack plane. In theory, the small plane is for bevels and end grain and the longer plane is better suited for flattening panels and edges, but sometimes it's the other way around. You'll also need some means of sharpening; oil stones, water stones, ceramic stones, or even sandpaper on glass will get the job done. A chunk of canning wax or the end of a candle is good for lubricating the plane's sole before you start work.

Add: A second "beater" block is handy for plywood and other carpentry tasks, followed by a second bench plane, such as a smaller #3 or larger #7. The size depends on the work

Planes to steer by. Handplanes provide a level of control and accuracy you won't find from power tools. Start out with a good block plane and a bench plane, then add additional tools to match your working style.

you do. Eventually, you may want to get a shoulder or rabbet plane for trimming tenons and a spokeshave for smoothing out curves.

Chisels

The problem with most chisels isn't the steel, but that they haven't been sharpened. A $40 starter set (¼", ½", ¾", and 1") will serve you well for years. Make or buy a mallet right away so that you're not tempted to use a metal hammer. Remember that chisels are consumables, like pencils. That said, even the most used chisel will last for a decade or two.

Add: As with planes, it helps to own a "beater" for slicing off dried glue, spreading wood filler, and so on. You'll want to keep this chisel sharp but not obsessively honed.

Keep it sharp. Using a sharpening jig, even beginners can hone chisels shaving-sharp. Sharpening with sandpaper on glass is a good way to start, but in the long run, water or oil stones will save you money.

Saws

In addition to the basic "carpentry" gear—crosscut saw, coping saw, and hacksaw—you'll want to get a dovetail saw and a flush-cut saw. To start, stick with a basic dovetail saw. As with planes and chisels, learning is less painful with less expensive tools. After a time, you'll discover whether you prefer pushing a western-type saw or pulling a Japanese-style saw, and you'll know what kind of saw to look for.

Clamps

While it may be impossible to own too many clamps, if you plan out your purchases, you can own enough to meet your needs 95 percent of the time. Start with a pair of 24" panel clamps for gluing boards into wider panels, a pair of lighter-duty bar clamps for smaller gluing chores, a few spring clamps for smaller projects and positioning stop blocks on your tablesaw and miter saw, and a toggle clamp for jigs. When you can afford to add to your collection, consider buying a pair that's a size larger than you need. For example, 48"-long panel clamps will work alongside your pair of 24" clamps, but they'll also provide extra reach for larger projects in the future.

Don't forget the bench vise. A permanent fixture on most workbenches, a bench vise transforms a basic tabletop into a valuable workshop companion. Used in tandem with bench dogs, the vise safely secures your work so that you can focus on routing, planing, and sawing.

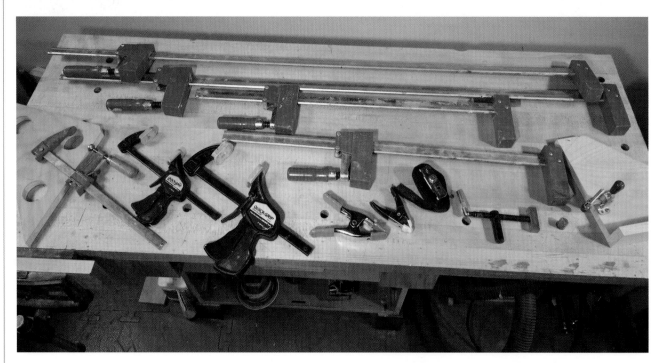

Clamping starter set. This basic collection of panel, bar, and spring clamps is enough to complete most of the projects in this book. And no bench would be complete without a vise and bench dogs.

Just add power. Power hand tools are well suited for the small shop because they can be stowed away when not in use. Remember to factor in the cost of bits, blades, disks, and biscuits.

Handheld Power Tools

Electric hand tools are a complement to, rather than a substitute for, the tools at the top of this list. For smaller tasks, you'll discover that you can do many things by hand in less time than it takes to unwind a cord; on the other hand, routers and biscuit jointers invite beginners to successfully accomplish projects with edging and joinery details that would take hours (and lots of practice) to accomplish by hand.

Once you become proficient with sanders, routers, and biscuit jointers, you'll move from the beginning to the end of a project more quickly. The sense of accomplishment allows you to progress to more challenging projects without unnecessary worry.

The tools displayed on this bench are all you need to tackle any of the projects in this book. If you don't have a particular tool, try a different technique or borrow the tool from a friend before heading to the store.

Sander

Random-orbit sanders remove stock almost as aggressively as belt sanders but are also capable of leaving a super-smooth finish. Combining rotary and orbital action, they can produce a scratch-free surface even when sanding across the grain. Larger 6" sanders are better for flattening larger surfaces, but smaller 5" general-purpose models are easier to handle. A 5" model can tackle almost any power-sanding task you'll encounter.

Drill

In woodworking, *cordless* translates to "one less cord to trip over." A 12- or 14-volt model should be more than sufficient for most woodworking tasks. If possible, look for a set that offers an extra battery and "smart" charger.

Add: Invest in a set of brad-point and Forstner bits for boring clean holes in wood. In addition to a pack of screwdriver bits, you'll want to pick up a countersink bit (buy both a ⅜" and ½") for setting screw heads below the surface of the wood and a centering bit for accurately drilling pilot holes in hinges and predrilled holes.

Router

A 1 to 1¾ hp. router is more than adequate for most edging and joinery tasks. Larger routers are capable of using bigger bits but are often built into router tables, because they're too unwieldy for certain handheld operations.

Add: A router is little more than a motor. To realize its full potential, you'll also need to invest in various bits, bushings, and guides. You'll find instructions for building a router table and several useful guides in future pages.

Circular saw

A circular saw is usually thought of as a carpentry tool, but for the times where your big machines can't make a cut, you'll discover how handy it is to have one in the shop. An entry-level saw should be more than adequate for the occasional plywood or panel cuts.

Add: The blade that comes with most saws is barely suited for slicing studs. Immediately replace it with a thin-kerf 32- or 40-tooth blade.

Biscuit jointer

Biscuit joinery is the fastest way to make strong mechanical joints in solid wood or plywood. All you need to do is plunge the tool's spinning cutter into mating workpieces, then glue in a flat, football-shaped biscuit made of compressed wood fibers. Unlike doweled joints, the shape of the slot and biscuit allow some "wiggle room" to correct less-than-perfect alignment, and the biscuit swells to lock the joint together when you apply glue. Biscuits really shine when making butt, corner, and miter joints. In these cases, this two-second joint can substitute for other joinery solutions that require more time or skill to accomplish.

Jigsaw

A jigsaw is more than just a small-tool substitute for a bandsaw. Not limited by throat depth, this portable tool can cut into workpieces of any length or width. Armed with an assortment of (relatively inexpensive) blades, it can slice through wood, laminate, tile, plastic, and metal. When shopping for a saw, look at those models that offer both straight-line and orbital blade action.

Larger Woodworking Machines

This section started out as "Stationary Machines," but in truth, few of the machines used in this book are truly stationary. For the beginner, benchtop tools are accurate and powerful enough to do fairly serious woodworking. The fact that they can also be rolled out of the way will enable you to make the most of a small shop.

Solid small-shop performers. A benchtop tablesaw will serve you well for years, but using one will also provide extra space and funds for other essential machines, such as a jointer, planer, and compressor.

Tablesaw

Benchtop models might not have the raw power of their bigger brothers, but they have the requisite accuracy and plenty of power to enable you to do some real woodworking. Buying a more affordable tool will also help you save up for a jointer and planer—the other two tools in the woodshop trinity.

Add: Buy a rip or combination blade (a good one will cost $50 to $100) and a dado set for cutting wide grooves and dadoes. If you do not yet own a jointer, consider buying a glue-line rip blade for ripping edges that are clean enough to be glued up into larger panels.

Planer

You'll soon discover that boards don't always come smooth and ready for assembly. When you've grown tired of paying extra to have your wood surfaced, or no longer want to build in ¾" increments, you may want to do the work yourself. A benchtop planer is perfect for smoothing rough-sawn lumber and milling it to uniform thickness.

It's important to note that planers are only good for making boards thinner; they're not designed to remove warp, twist, or cup from a board. To straighten boards, you'll need to flatten one face on a jointer or with a handplane.

Jointer

Woodworking demands square, straight edges and flat surfaces. There are ways to use jigs or hand tools to meet these requirements, but few methods are as fast as a jointer. The size of a jointer is based on its maximum width of cut. While jointers are made in sizes up to 24", 6" and 8" models are more suited for small shops.

Compressor

At one time, large tanks were seen only in professional shops. These days, small, affordable air compressors are common in many small workshops. You'll really appreciate a compressor's convenience when you couple it with a few pneumatic tools. Unlike the hammer-and-nail approach, air nailers allow you to hold the piece with one hand and fasten it with the other. The smaller fasteners are less likely to split the wood. Your compressor may also be able to power a spray gun, which will enable you to quickly apply finish to large surfaces. In the future, you may decide to invest in larger framing nailers, small staplers, or various other air-powered tools.

Safety

They say that woodworking is inherently dangerous, but the trick is to understand what the risks are. For example, not using guards at every opportunity increases the risk of losing a finger, but it doesn't necessarily condemn you to it. Not using ear or lung protection, on the other hand, is a fool's bet. You may not notice any problems now, but you will suffer from the effects of your carelessness years down the road. Buy—and use—the appropriate protective gear. If you have regular shop helpers, invest in extra equipment. You may also consider asking visitors to leave if you're doing something that might jeopardize their health, or if the distraction of having them around might endanger yours.

Accidents still happen. For little scrapes and cuts, keep a small first-aid kit handy. Add a bottle of peroxide and eyewash solution to the basic kit. The phone is for anything bigger than a Band-Aid™. You may never need to use a fire extinguisher, but with wood, electricity, and chemicals in such close contact, you should have one handy, just in case.

A safe investment. Whether it's needed for everyday use or a single worst-case scenario, you can't be without standard safety gear. Buy the basics and make sure they're always within reach.

Desk Organizer

So much for those predictions of a "paperless society." Despite the digital revolution, most desks are still buried under a flurry of documents, sticky notes, and miscellaneous office supplies. Sometimes we have to relocate to the kitchen table. If this sounds all too familiar, then this project might be the perfect office mate. This desk organizer is a great tool for making sense of everyday office chaos—for holding paper, pens, a pocket calendar, your checkbook, and a calculator . . . even stationery, for those times when an e-mail just won't cut it. This project can also serve as a handy kitchen organizer. The vertical dividers are great for sorting bills and coupons, for stashing recipes, or for gathering phone messages until you can return a call. Few other projects work as hard and use so little wood.

Beginning and experienced woodworkers alike can appreciate a warm-up project every now and then. This project should only take two or three days to complete. If you haven't spent much time in the shop lately, or at all, consider this as an opportunity to sharpen your planes and chisels and hone your power- and hand-tool skills. Spending a few hours improving your shop and having more to show for your efforts than just a few bags of sawdust can be nice for a change.

While this project can be rewarding by itself, it's intended to serve as a launching pad for this book. As you build this project, you'll learn new techniques and be introduced to a few jigs that will make future projects easier and more enjoyable. For example, the benchtop router table—a stand-alone mini-project—is perfect for quickly chamfering or rounding edges, even if you own a full-sized model. In this chapter, you'll learn how to use a cabinet scraper, a tool you'll continue to reach for on future projects.

Now let's get started.

What You'll Learn

- **Jointing an edge**
- **Using a cabinet scraper**
- **Strategies for staining and finishing**
- **Cutting dadoes and grooves with a tablesaw**
- **Chamfering edges with a router**
- **Fitting a drawer**

Jointing with a shooting board. Using this set up, you can safely joint boards that might be too short for an electric jointer.

You don't need to build all of the projects in the order that they appear in this book, but this is a great project to begin with if you're just starting out. As you build this desk organizer, you'll learn different strategies for working with—and sometimes around—the tools you already own. For example, if you don't yet own a jointer, you'll learn how to use a tablesaw and a handplane to joint edges safely and quickly to make wider panels. You'll also build a simple router table that is likely to become a go-to tool in your shop. Of course, you may discover that you don't really need to make any upgrades and can now focus your attention on entirely different tools (or perhaps just buy more wood).

This chapter will also introduce you to a few techniques that will come in handy when tackling future projects. You'll learn how to cut tight-fitting dadoes and grooves—a task you'll encounter repeatedly as a woodworker—as well as familiarize yourself with the process of gluing up assemblies. Building a simple, false-front drawer is a skill you can use on any case piece featuring drawers. And once you try staining before assembly, you may never again think of finishing as the final step.

Scrapers make shavings, not dust. Once you learn how to tune them, you'll use scrapers for everything from knocking off dried glue to smoothing figured wood.

Fitting a false-front drawer. To make drawers that fit like a piston, forget measuring with a ruler. Reach for a marking knife and mark directly off the case.

A Simple Desk Organizer

Made from ¼" and ½" stock, this handy desk organizer is a good primer for tablesawn joinery and an introduction to hand-tool skills you'll use in later chapters.

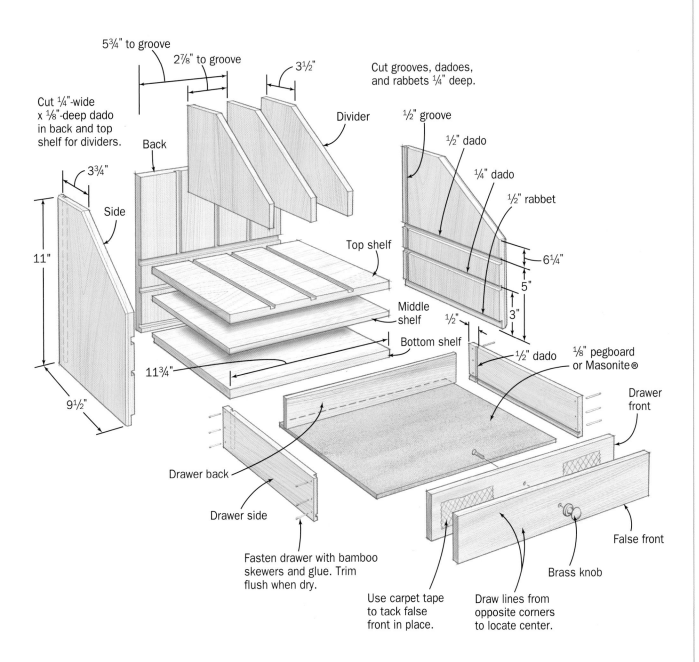

5¾" to groove

2⅞" to groove

3½"

Cut grooves, dadoes, and rabbets ¼" deep.

Cut ¼"-wide x ⅛"-deep dado in back and top shelf for dividers.

Back

Divider

½" groove

½" dado

¼" dado

½" rabbet

3¾"

Side

Top shelf

6¼"

11"

5"

Middle shelf

½"

3"

Bottom shelf

½" dado

⅛" pegboard or Masonite®

11¾"

Drawer front

9½"

Drawer back

Drawer side

False front

Brass knob

Fasten drawer with bamboo skewers and glue. Trim flush when dry.

Use carpet tape to tack false front in place.

Draw lines from opposite corners to locate center.

Quantity	Part	Actual Size	Note
2	Sides	½" x 9½" x 10⅝"	Oak
1	Bottom	½" x 9½" x 11¾"	Oak
1	Middle shelf	¼" x 9" x 11¾"	Oak
1	Top shelf	½" x 9" x 11¾"	Oak
1	Back	¼" x 11¾" x 10⅝"	At 10⅝", it's a little wider than needed. Plane to fit after assembly.
3	Vertical dividers	¼" x 9" x 6⅛"	Leave board longer than needed. Trim to fit assembled case.
1	False drawer front	¼" x 2³⁄₁₆" x 11¼"	Oak
2	Drawer sides	¼" x 2³⁄₁₆" x 8¾"	Poplar or pine. These dimensions are slightly oversized. Trim to fit once the case is assembled.
2	Drawer front and back	¼" x 2³⁄₁₆" x 11"	Poplar or pine. Trim to fit once the case is assembled.
1	Drawer bottom	⅛" x 9" x 11"	Hardboard or Masonite
	Bamboo skewers		To reinforce the drawer corner joints
1	Drawer lining	8" x 10¾"	You can use matte board alone or felt attached to cardboard.
1	Small brass knob		
	Stain		Optional—to even out or add additional color
	Carpet tape		For temporarily attaching false front to drawer
	Wiping varnish		1 pint is plenty.
	Miscellaneous		Paste wax, white synthetic abrasive pad, tack cloth, spray adhesive, rags, 220-grit sandpaper

Buying Materials

If you built this piece from ¾"-thick material, it would not only look clunky, but it also would leave little space between the boards to do any organizing. In the past, only woodworkers who owned planers and jointers were able to build with thinner stock. For those who don't yet own such equipment, you can now buy ¼"- and ½"-thick stock at your local home center. Most home centers offer a small supply of thin poplar, oak, and maple. If you prefer another species, you can also order thin stock online (see Sources on p. 170).

When choosing boards, select the flattest boards you can find. All wood moves in response to changes in humidity, but thin boards may begin to bow quite dramatically in a relatively short period of time. You may

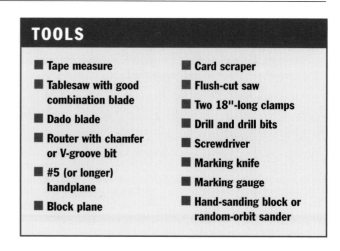

be able to correct minor bowing or cupping during assembly, but the time you spend selecting straight boards now will save lots of frustration later. Before you buy, arrange the boards side by side to make sure that the color and grain matches reasonably well.

Building the Desk Organizer

Building the Case

Whether it happens at the lumberyard or while being tossed around in your own lumber racks, the edges of boards can get pretty beaten up. Before starting any project, it's a good idea to trim all the factory edges at the tablesaw. Before cutting your stock to exact size, trim the boards so that they're at least ¼" wider than what's shown on the materials list. This way, you can cut a little off one edge, flip the board, then rip it to width. Doing this ensures that both edges are square and undamaged.

If you can't find lumber as wide as what's listed in the materials list, you'll need to glue up two or more boards to make the sides, shelves, and dividers. Being able to seamlessly glue edge joints is one of the first woodworking skills you'll need to master. You may not yet own an electric jointer, but even if you do, there are times where a board may be too long or too short to joint safely, which is why it makes sense to know a few alternative techniques. Below, I'll show you how to joint boards using a handplane, but you can achieve the same end with a tablesaw (for more on this process, see "Skill Builder: Jointing Edges on a Tablesaw" on p. 21).

Whatever method you use, remember to play around with the boards before gluing them up. Experiment with the grain and orient boards so that each blends with the next, then mark the faces accordingly.

Make wide boards from narrow ones

Jointing small stock so you'll have a crisp, square edge is actually safer and easier (and quieter) to do by hand than machine. To do this, you'll need a well-tuned plane with a nicely sharpened blade. Don't worry if you haven't yet developed a solid planing technique; the shooting board shown here makes the process easy to master (see photo A at right).

1. Lay both boards on a piece of ¾" plywood, then clamp or screw stops against the end and far edge of the boards so that the edge you want to joint sticks out by ¼".

Shooting an edge. Keeping the side of the plane flat against the bench ensures a perpendicular cut. For a seamless joint, plane two boards at once, then "fold" the jointed edges together.

Cauls keep glue-ups flat. When gluing boards edge to edge, use scraps of wood as cauls and clamp them across the width of the assembly. Tighten the clamps across the edge joint first, then clamp down on the cauls.

2. Resting the side of your plane against your benchtop, run (or "shoot") the plane against the two boards. "Folding" boards at the joint line, clamping them together, and planing both at once ensures that the edges match up (see the drawing below). Any variation from a perfect 90° angle on the first board will be offset by the complementary angle you planed on the second. If the planed edge seems rough, or if your plane chatters while making the cut, you may be trying to plane against the grain. Try planing the board in the opposite direction.

3. Edge glue and clamp the pieces together as shown in photo B, using cauls to keep the panels flat. Apply blue painter's tape or packing tape to the cauls to so that they don't get glued to the panels accidentally.

Two Wrongs Can Make a Right

The scrap wood shooting board, as shown on p. 19, is designed for use with a handplane. It can be used to joint two edges at once. If you "fold" the boards, as shown at right, your plane will create complementary angles on the edges of the two boards. In other words, the boards will match up even if the plane's blade is not perfectly perpendicular to your workbench.

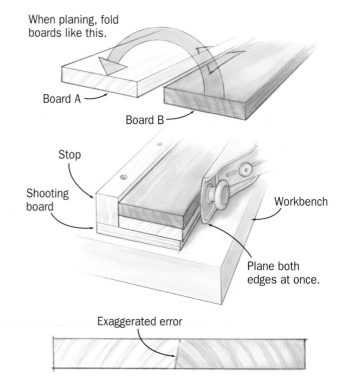

When planing, fold boards like this.

Board A

Board B

Stop

Shooting board

Workbench

Plane both edges at once.

Exaggerated error

Sizing your stock

It's best to remove any stains or mill marks before you cut the parts to size. Your stock may suffer a few minor dents or scratches later on, but it's too easy to accidentally round over the edges of small pieces when sanding a finished project. Plus, once the case is assembled, it will be difficult to fit your fingers, much less a sander, between the dividers or shelves.

Before sanding, scrape off any dried glue with a card scraper. (For more on tuning and using a card scraper, see "Skill Builder: Using a Cabinet Scraper" on pp. 22–23.) Next, lightly scrape or plane both sides of your stock, as shown in photo C on p. 24. If you prefer, you

WORK SMART

If thin stock is cupped, try sponging a little water onto the concave side. Moisture on this face will cause the fibers to expand, maybe enough to flatten the board. The water will also raise the grain, but that can be quickly remedied with a light sanding. Finishing prevents future movement.

could also use a sander with 220-grit sandpaper (if you have to sand out deeper scratches, start with 150-grit or 120-grit sandpaper, then work up to the finer paper).

SKILL BUILDER: Jointing Edges on a Tablesaw

What You'll Need

- **Tablesaw**
- **Combination square**
- **Quality rip or combination blade (preferably carbide tipped)**

If you've taken time to properly set your tablesaw and have a decent blade, you can get a finished edge that's nearly as good as what you might get from a jointer. First, use a combination square to make sure that the blade is perpendicular to the table. Next, set the rip fence so that the blade will shave only the edge of the board. Making sure that the board stays in contact with the fence, rip the first board (with the good side facing up) along the joint line. Now remembering your complementary angles, flip the next board so

Joint edges with a tablesaw. Both edges of the joint will be lightly cut by the sawblade: one face up, the other face down. For the smoothest cut, a featherboard can help keep the wood against the fence.

that the good side is facing down and make your cut. When the two boards go together, any slight variation from 90° will be offset by the complementary angle on the mating board.

What You'll Need

- **Cabinet scraper**
- **Fine mill file**
- **Sharpening stone**
- **Burnisher (screwdriver, drill bit, or hinge pin)**
- **Bench vise**

I'm convinced that the sandpaper companies have conspired against this simple piece of steel. Why else would a technique that's so simple, effective, and inexpensive be seen as some sort of lost art? Burnishing a scraper is no more difficult than setting up a tablesaw, and it's faster than driving to the hardware store to buy another pack of sandpaper. Unlike sandpaper, a scraper can be adjusted to make coarse or fine cuts. In addition, that $5 scraper will last a lifetime.

You can scrape by without a lot of equipment. If you don't own a burnisher, you can use a high-speed drill bit or the shank side of a broken carbide router bit.

1. Some new scrapers come with perfectly machined edges (allowing you to omit this step), but even so, you will eventually need to square the edge. To do this, clamp the scraper in a vise and flatten the edge with

a fine mill file. File until you can see a uniformly fresh edge on your scraper.

Alternately, you make this filing jig (see photo A). Use your tablesaw to cut a groove that's the same width as your file. If the groove's a little too wide, attach masking tape to the back face of the file to hold it in place.

2. Use your sharpening stone and hold the scraper upright to hone the edge. (Move the scraper around as you're doing this, otherwise you will wear a groove in your stone.) After honing the edge, hone both sides. Place the steel face down on the stone and rub in a circular motion (see photo B).

You can try out your scraper at this point. Some woodworkers use scrapers with

A

B

a squared, honed edge for fine-finishing tasks, such as slicing off drips or dust nibs from dried finishes.

3. To draw the edge, lay the scraper flat on your bench and draw the burnisher along the top. It might not seem like you're doing anything, but drawing hardens the edge so that the burr will last longer (see the drawing at right). Lean into the stroke so that you're putting some weight behind the burnisher. (Later, when your scraper starts to dull, you can redraw the edge and roll a fresh burr a couple of times before going all the way back to step 1.) Flip the scraper over and draw the opposite face (see photo C).

4. To roll the burr, clamp the scraper in a vise. Hold the burnisher perpendicular to the scraper and run it along the edge (see photo D). Make two or three more strokes, each time tilting the burnisher until it's at about a 15° angle (see the drawing at right). Repeat this step in the other direction to create a hook on both sides of the edge.

When turning a burr, less is more. Too steep an angle or too much pressure on the burnisher will create a heavy burr that will quickly bend back or snap off completely. If

Tuning Up a Scraper

A scraper is first filed and honed so that the edge is square to the faces (A), then drawn to flatten a burr on the edge (B). Finally, the burr (basically, a hook) is turned with a burnisher, creating a cutting edge (C).

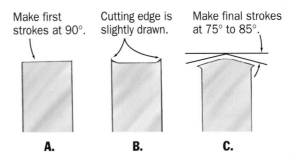

Make first strokes at 90°.

Cutting edge is slightly drawn.

Make final strokes at 75° to 85°.

A. **B.** **C.**

the hardened steel burnisher were a yellow No. 2 pencil, your burnishing pressure shouldn't be enough to snap the pencil in two.

5. A scraper can be used on either the push or pull stroke. Either way, tilt the blade until the hook catches and start scraping. You'll find that flexing the blade will help keep the corners from digging in. Cocking the scraper at an angle to the grain helps it smooth, instead of magnify, mill marks.

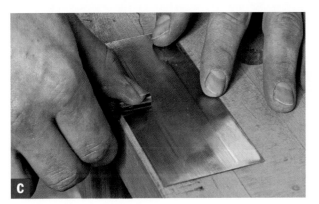

C

D

Using a card scraper. Gently flex the scraper with your thumbs and tilt the blade until the hook catches the wood. Be sure to scrape the whole surface evenly; if you get carried away in one spot, you'll create a dip.

1. Rip all of the stock for the case to width. (Don't cut the pieces for the drawer yet; they'll be cut to fit into the drawer opening after you have assembled the basic case.) To avoid fence-setting errors, set your saw once, then rip all the pieces that should be cut to that dimension. First, rip the sides and the bottom 9½" wide. Next, rip the wood for the dividers at 9⅛", and then the top and middle shelves at 9". Finally, rip a piece at 10⅝" for the back panel.

2. At this point, it's a good idea to label your material to help you remember what is used where. You can write on pieces of masking tape or directly on the wood itself. Place your label on the best side of each board, and remember to orient the wood so that the best side is facing outward during subsequent steps.

3. Crosscut your pieces to length, as shown in photo D. Again, cut all pieces that are the same length at the same time to avoid measurement-related errors. Using your tablesaw or a miter saw, cut the bottom, shelf, and back pieces to 11¾" long. Crosscut the sides to 10⅝". Finally, cut the three dividers to 6⅛".

Stop blocks are more exact than pencil lines. Measure the first board, then clamp a block to your miter saw's fence to ensure that each piece will be the same length.

Making the sides and dividers

E

Planing two boards at once. **A freshly sharpened block plane is great for shaving off saw marks. Clamp the two sides together so that the boards remain identical.**

1. Once all pieces are cut to length, set your miter saw to cut a 45° miter, and nip one corner off both sides and the front top corner of the three vertical dividers. If your miter saw lacks the capacity to make the full cut, flip the board over and finish the cut from the opposite end or use a handsaw. To smooth out the two-step cut, clamp the sides in your bench vise, then use your block plane. Remember to plane downhill—in this case from the front edge toward the top end, as shown in photo E. Be careful not to tear out the wood at the end of the cut.

2. Chamfer the outside edges of the side panels at the router table. Remember that the sides are mirror images, not identical. Establish a "right" and "left" side and chamfer only the top and two outside edges. One way to help remember the correct orientation

> **WORK SMART**
>
> **R**outers tend to tear out chunks of wood when cutting end grain. One way to work around this is to rout the ends first, then the edges. The second pass should clean up any splinters made by the first.

is to tack the pieces together with double-sided carpet tape before routing, as shown in photo F. If you'd prefer, you can cut the chamfers with a block plane, but this router table will earn its keep in future projects. To learn how to make a simple bench-mounted router table, refer to "Skill Builder: Making a Simple Router Table" on pp. 28–29.

3. It may seem premature, but you'll find it a lot easier to finish the pieces now, before they are assembled into small shelves and tight compartments. Lightly sand all surfaces

F

Chamfer the edges. **Adjust the fence to cut a ¼"-high bevel on the outside face of the front, back, and mitered end of both sides. Taping the boards together prevents you from forgetting that there's a left and right side.**

by hand with 220-grit sandpaper. If you want a darker color, or need to even out different-colored boards, you can apply stain (see photo G). Once the stain has dried, apply two coats of a wipe-on varnish. The varnish will help seal and protect the wood without creating a thick plastic look.

4. Replace your tablesaw blade with a dado cutter and set it to cut a ¼"-wide by ¼"-deep dado. On a piece of scrap, make a test cut and try fitting the middle shelf into the practice groove. Adjust the dado cutter for a fit that's snug, but not so tight that you need to hammer it together. Once you have a good fit, set the rip fence and cut the dadoes in both sides for the middle shelf. Next, reset the fence and cut the groove for the back panel.

5. To cut the dadoes for the ½"-thick bottom and top shelves, you could adjust the width of the dado cutter, but doing so would mean removing the dado, inserting shims to establish the correct dado width, and then re-establishing the exact depth of the dadoes you've just cut. A faster and easier way to make the two ½"-wide dadoes for the shelves

and ½"-wide rabbet for the bottom is by making them in two passes with the narrower cutter already installed on your saw. Mark the location of the top shelf and bottom on the leading edge of one of the sides. Carefully work up to your line, as shown in photo H below. It's better to make three passes than to take off too much in one pass.

When cutting grooves or dadoes along outside ends or edges—a cut called a rabbet—

G

Think finish first. Applying stain is easier before assembly, especially if the first coat reveals a rough spot that you might have missed when sanding. For a good color match, some boards might require a second coat.

H

Dado and rabbet the sides. Replace your sawblade with a dado cutter to cut the dadoes for the shelves and rabbet for the bottom. Use a plywood auxiliary fence whenever you're cutting up to the edge or end of a board.

attach a sacrificial piece of plywood or medium-density fiberboard (MDF) to your rip fence. Doing this not only keeps your dado cutter safely away from the fence, it also enables you to "bury" the cutter into the fence. This enables you to cut narrower grooves along the edge without removing and resetting the cutter.

6. After making all of the ¼"-deep cuts, lower the dado cutter and cut the ⅛"-deep grooves for the dividers. Again, make a test cut to ensure a tight fit. Note that the grooves are in the same location on the back and top shelves. If you groove the top shelf and then cut the matching groove in the back before resetting the fence, both grooves will line up perfectly when you assemble the case.

Assemble the case

You're now ready to attach the sides to the shelves. To avoid headaches, dry-assemble the case first, before applying any glue. A practice run gives you a chance to correct small mistakes before they become a sticky mess. You may also need to sand or plane the edges a little to help them slide into place. Once a thorough dry-fitting has ironed out any wrinkles in the process, you're ready to glue up.

WORK SMART

Regular yellow glues require you to work fairly fast; most have a 5-minute working time. If you think you might need more assembly time, consider using liquid hide glue or a yellow glue with an "extended" working time. Either will give you up to 20 minutes to set the last clamp.

1. Using a thin scrap of wood or small brush, apply a small amount of glue to all the grooves in the sides. Position the bottom and both shelves between the sides, gently clamp the case together, then slide in the back panel. Tighten the clamps, then check the assembly to make sure it's square (see photo at right). To ensure that the glue has cured, give the assembly about one hour before removing the clamps.

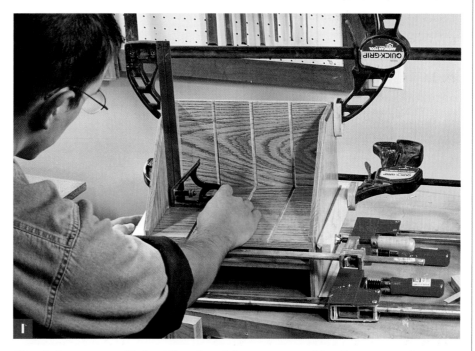

Check for square. Before the glue dries, use a combination square to make sure the assembly is square. Realize that clamps aren't a cure-all; overclamping can pull a perfectly good project out of whack.

What You'll Need

- ■ **Router**
- ■ **Straight bit**
- ■ **¾" by 9" by 16" piece of plywood**
- ■ **¾" by 2" by 6" piece of plywood**
- ■ **¾" by 2" by 16" pine board**
- ■ **⅜" countersink (see Sources on p. 170)**
- ■ **Glue**
- ■ **1¼" drywall screws**
- ■ **Screwdriver**
- ■ **Clamps**

R outers are one of the few shop tools that are equally as useful upside down as they are right-side up. In fact, if you have a large router, or are trying to shape short stock, turning your portable router into a stationary machine may make things easier and safer. The thing to remember is that router tables need not be big or fancy to be effective. This router table takes up just a square foot of space, but it's perfect for shaping edges or routing grooves up to 4" from the edge of a board.

1. Cut the piece of ¾" plywood to make the base. If you have a larger piece of plywood, consider making the top a few inches wider. You can always trim the base after construction.

2. The next step is to determine the location of the router. To do this, position the base on top of your bench so that all but 2" hangs off the edge and clamp it in place. Next, place your router on top of the base so that, if it were hanging underneath, it would clear the edge of your bench or any other obstacles. Trace the outline of the router's base on the board (see photo A).

3. Using your router and a straight bit, rout out the ⅜"-deep mortise, as shown in photo B, to house the baseplate. It's okay to rout the recess freehand; it doesn't have to fit the base perfectly. The goal is simply to remove enough wood so that you can reuse the short baseplate screws to attach the router to the plywood.

Position the router. To lay out the location for the mortise, place your router on the plywood and trace around your router's base.

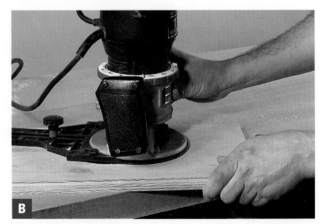

Mortise for the base. Here a ¼"-diameter straight bit and circle-cutting guide that came with this router are used, but you can also make the cut freehand.

A Quick and Easy Router Table

Inverting a router in a table enables you to cut various joinery that can't be cut with a router held upright. Building this table calls for only a scrap of plywood and a few short boards.

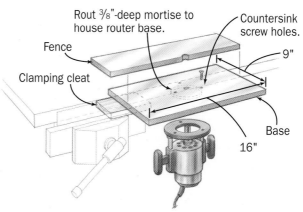

Rout ⅜"-deep mortise to house router base.

Countersink screw holes.

Fence

Clamping cleat

9"

Base

16"

4. Place your router in the mortise, then mark the locations of the baseplate's screw holes to the plywood. Using a bit slightly larger than the diameter of the screws, drill through the plywood. Next, working from the top, countersink the holes so that the screw heads will sit below the surface of the plywood (see photo C).

5. Fasten your router to the base and place it back on your bench. You can now mark out the location and size of the cleat that will be held by your bench vise. Attach the cleat with screws and glue.

6. To make the hole in the base for the bit, you can turn on your router and slowly raise the bit through the plywood (see photo D). If you plan to use a bit that has a bearing on its tip, you'll need to remove the base and drill a starter hole. If you have a plunge router, flip the base over so that you can use both hands to lower the router.

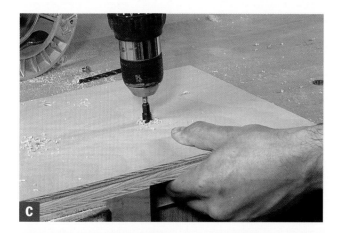

C

Sinking the screws. Use the ⅜" counterbore to sink the screw heads so that they won't interfere with workpieces. If you're working with short screws, you may need to drill even deeper holes.

D

First cut. Slowly advance your router's depth adjustment so the bit can cut a hole for itself through the plywood base.

2. Using a block or bench plane, plane down the top edge of the back piece so that it lies flush with the tops of the sides as shown in photo J. Next, test-fit dividers into the organizer case. If necessary, trim the tops of the dividers before they're glued in place. Once everything fits, apply glue to the grooves in the back and top shelf, then slide the vertical dividers in place.

Plane it flush. Your block plane is the tool for sneaking up on a perfect fit. Use the sides and a temporarily installed divider as planing guides.

Building the Drawer

Because this drawer is so small, and probably won't suffer the same use and abuse as the silverware drawer in your kitchen, you can use fairly simple joinery. The following instructions walk you through the process of building drawers that are simply rabbeted and dadoed boxes with false drawer fronts glued on. If you prefer an easier route, you can make a serviceable drawer by simply butt-joining the front and back to the sides; since the bottom is glued in place, a little glue and bamboo skewers (used in place of nails) on the corners is enough to hold it together. In either case, use the dimensions given in the materials list as a guide only. The goal is to fit the drawer to the case, not to make cuts just because the cut list tells you to.

1. Using the organizer as your guide, rip stock for the front, back, and sides of the drawers. Test the fit against the case and size it so that the stock slides smoothly into the drawer cavity (see photo A).

2. On the front and two sides, cut a ⅛"-deep groove to house the drawer bottom. Instead of grooving the back, raise the blade and trim away the groove completely.

WORK SMART

For a flat-bottomed saw kerf, switch over to a rip blade. Alternately, you can use one of the chippers from your dado set.

Smooth sliding sides. Measurements provide some guidance, but nothing beats the real thing. Cut the drawer sides so that they fit the opening with just a little wiggle room.

Mark the front. Butt the front of the drawer against one drawer side, then mark the opposite end of the front.

3. Crosscut the sides so that they are ¼" shorter than the depth of the drawer opening.

4. Place a single side piece into the opening and use it as a spacer to determine the length of the front and back pieces. Set the drawer front in place and make a small mark with a knife or fine-tipped pencil, as shown in photo B. After cutting the rabbets (in the front) and dadoes (in the back) on the sides, the front will fit in the opening between both sides. As you crosscut the front and back pieces, "lose the line," or cut it a hair short. That way, the drawer will have a little room to move from side to side.

5. Use a marking gauge to transfer the thickness of the drawer front to the front inside face of one of the drawer sides. Next, adjust your tablesaw to make a ⅛"-deep cut and adjust your rip fence so that the blade is

cutting along the inside front face of the drawer side (see photo C). It may take two or three passes to nibble up to the end of the

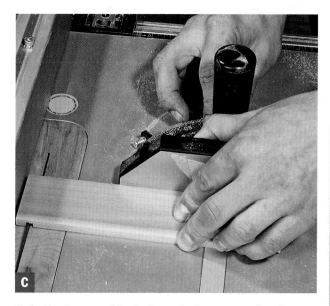

Substitute a sawblade for a dado cutter. Cutting the grooves and rabbets on the drawer sides with a single blade is faster than switching over to a dado cutter, even if it takes a few passes.

board, but this is faster than switching to a dado cutter. Repeat this cut on the inside front end of the other side piece.

6. To cut the dado to house the back of the drawer, adjust the fence so that there is ¼" between the fence and the blade, then pass the stock across the blade and make the mirror cut in the other side piece. Move the fence

another ⅛" away from the blade and take another pass. Sneak up on the proper fit slowly by making small adjustments to the fence. Test the drawer back in the dado until you have a good fit.

7. Dry-fit the drawer sides, front, and back, then measure the dimension of the bottom panel and cut it to fit.

Assemble the drawer

1. Apply glue to the corners and bottom grooves, then reassemble the drawer and check for square.

2. To provide extra reinforcement, "nail" each corner with bamboo skewers. Using a bit that's the same diameter as your skewers, drill three ½"-deep holes at each corner. (For additional mechanical strength, try to drill the holes at a slight angle.) Apply glue to the skewer and lightly tap it in place. When dry, trim the skewer flush to the side with a small saw or chisel (see photo D).

3. Find the center of the drawer front and drill a pilot hole for the small brass knob. The easiest way to do this is to use a straightedge

WORK SMART

To tack the false front to the drawer, use two small pieces of double-stick tape in addition to glue. The tape will hold the front in place until the glue dries.

and draw two lines connecting opposite corners (see photo E). The intersection of these two lines is the center.

4. Cut the false front to the exact size of the drawer opening. Attach the false front to the drawer, then drill from the back face of the drawer front through the false front. Insert the knob's mating machine screw in the hole and attach the knob.

D

Skewering the drawer. **Drill a hole and drive a bamboo skewer in place. Trim it flush to the surface after the glue has dried.**

E

X marks the spot. **The simplest way to find the center of your drawer is to draw lines connecting opposite corners.**

Finishing

You may need to do a few minor touchups to the finish at this point. Break any sharp edges with a block plane set for a very light cut, or a sanding block and 220-grit sandpaper. Use an extra-fine (white) abrasive pad to knock off any bumps that might have been left from earlier coats of finish. Wipe the surfaces with a tack cloth, then wipe again using a rag moistened with mineral spirits. Now you're ready to lay on your final coat of finish.

1. Apply a final coat of varnish to all the exterior surfaces (see photo A). And because you've prefinished all the parts, focus only on the outermost surfaces—don't worry if you can't reach into all of the narrow drawers and compartments. If you notice any other scuffs, conceal them by dabbing on a thin coat of varnish, waiting 10 minutes, then wiping off any excess.

2. Wait a day or so for the finish to cure, then apply a little paste wax with another

small scrap of abrasive pad. When the wax hazes over, polish it with a soft cloth. If you wait too long, you may have a difficult time buffing the wax. If this happens, apply more wax (to soften the first coat), and start buffing as soon as the wax starts getting a little cloudy.

3. You'll want to cover up the pegboard you used for the drawer bottom. To make a felt liner, cut a thin piece of cardboard to the inside dimensions of the drawer. Give the cardboard a spritz of spray adhesive and lay it face down on the felt. Trim the felt with a utility knife as shown in photo B, and drop the liner into the drawer.

A fine finish. An oil-varnish blend is enough to protect the piece from most spills, plus, the finish can be quickly and easily applied with a rag.

Details make the difference. Finish the drawer with a simple felt lining. Cut a piece of cardboard to fit snugly in the bottom, then cover it with felt and trim off any excess.

Blanket Box

At some point, every woodworker is asked to build a blanket or hope chest. Dating back to a time when a person might store their finest clothes and other possessions in one treasured box, these chests are still given as gifts at life's milestones, such as births and weddings. The problem with blanket chests is that too often they lose the battle for bedroom floor space. Traditionally, these chests were big pieces of furniture, 30" to 40" wide and up to 36" tall. In truth, most aren't as practical as a basic dresser or well-organized closet.

This project retains the blanket chest charm but takes up only a fraction of the footprint. Inspired by several different Shaker pieces, I halved the dimensions of a traditional chest. This miniature is nicely suited for storing knitting materials, CDs, or jewelry. Unlike a full-size version, this box can be a gift that will fit in the recipient's house, not to mention the car.

Making a half-scale reproduction of a classic design gives you the opportunity to practice the same joinery, but you'll use less wood. The smaller boards are also easier to handle on benchtop tools and in a smaller shop.

What You'll Learn

- **Resawing wood on the tablesaw**
- **Using a crosscut sled**
- **Cutting grooves and rabbets with a router**
- **Making a half-lap back**
- **Drawing fair curves**
- **Installing hinges**
- **Making a raised-panel drawer bottom**
- **Finishing with milk paint**

Mortising hinges. Learn how to install hinges that look like they've grown there. All you need is a chisel and a sharp knife.

In the first project, you used your tablesaw to cut the boards to dimension and for simple joinery. Although effective and accurate, the tablesaw isn't always the most efficient choice of tools. Switching back and forth from blade to dado cutter, then resetting the fence and cutting height, takes time. For that reason, you may want to consider using another tool. When armed with a few straight bits and set into a table, your router can cut rabbets, dadoes, and grooves just as accurately as your tablesaw. By the time you've completed this project, you'll understand both methods well enough so that for future projects, you will be able to choose the method that's most efficient.

Your tablesaw will still get a workout on this project. First, you'll learn how to make your own thin stock by resawing thick boards. You'll also learn how to make a crosscut sled to help you cut wide boards accurately on your tablesaw. Unlike the rickety miter gauge that comes with most saws, a crosscut sled is rock solid and always ready to make perfectly square cuts.

This project will also give you the opportunity to sharpen your hand-tool skills. You'll use a block plane to fine-tune the beveled drawer bottom and chamfer edges. Last but not least, you'll have an opportunity to try milk paint. Milk paint is easy to apply, is quick to dry, and looks better as it ages. It's the perfect finishing technique when you want to add color to a project built from common pine or a plain-grained hardwood.

Milk paint magic. Milk paint is as easy to make as pancake mix, brushes on like ordinary latex, but produces a museum-quality finish. It's perfect for spicing up plain pine or poplar.

New Size for a Classic Design

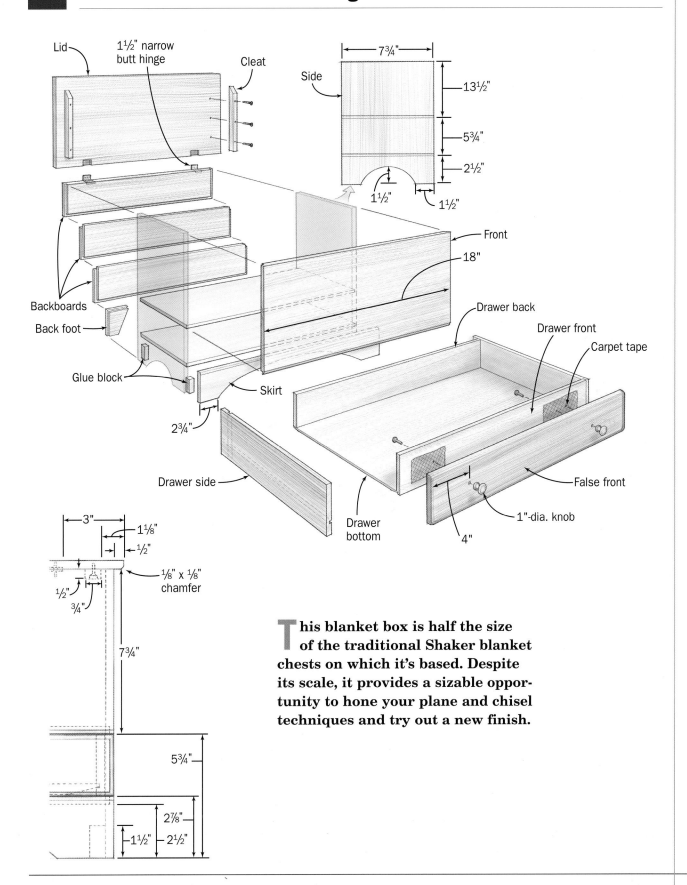

Lid

1½" narrow butt hinge

Cleat

Side

7¾"

13½"

5¾"

2½"

1½"

1½"

Front

18"

Backboards

Back foot

Drawer back

Drawer front

Carpet tape

Glue block

Skirt

2¾"

Drawer side

Drawer bottom

False front

1"-dia. knob

4"

3"

1⅛"

½"

⅛" x ⅛" chamfer

½"

¾"

7¾"

5¾"

2⅞"

1½"

2½"

This blanket box is half the size of the traditional Shaker blanket chests on which it's based. Despite its scale, it provides a sizable opportunity to hone your plane and chisel techniques and try out a new finish.

Quantity	Part	Actual Size	Notes
2	Sides	⅜" x 7¾" x 13½"	You can build this entire box from one 5/4" x 9" x 72" board, but you may want to buy a little extra wood, just in case.
2	Bottoms	⅜" x 7¾" x 17⅝"	Top board will be ripped to 7⅜" to fit between front and back boards.
1	Front	⅜" x 7⅝" x 18"	Start with 8"-wide top and trim to fit after building box.
1	Skirt	⅜" x 2¾" x 18"	
3	Back boards	⅜" x 4" x 18"	Depending on the spacing between boards, you may need to plane the top board flush with the top edge of box.
2	Back feet	⅜" x 2⅞" x 4¼"	To keep fingers safely away from the blade, cut feet from one 2⅞" x 10" board.
1	Lid	⅜" x 8⅝" x 19"	
2	Cleats	½" x ¾" x 7"	
2	Drawer sides	⅜" x 2¾" x 7⅜"	Sides should slide easily into drawer opening of assembled case.
1	Drawer front	⅜" x 2¾" x 16¾"	
1	Drawer back	⅜" x 2¼" x 16¾"	
1	Drawer bottom	⅜" x 7¼" x 16¾"	
1	Drawer false front	¼" x 2¾" x 18"	¼"-thick false front sits flush with ⅜"-thick front and skirt.
4	Glue blocks	¾" x ¾" x 1½"	
2	1"-dia. knobs		Brass, cast steel, or wood would all look good. Consider oiling wood knobs to contrast painted box.
3	Small brass box hinges	1½" x ⅝" 1¾"	
	#6 pan head screw		For attaching drawer bottom to drawer back
6	⅝" #4 wood screws		
	⅝" brads		Buy a box—you'll need leftovers for later projects.
	Milk paint		See Sources on p. 170
	2" bristle brush		An inexpensive disposable brush works fine.
	Wiping varnish		
	Miscellaneous		Yellow glue, latex wood putty, double-sided tape, paste wax, 180-grit and 220-grit sandpaper, 000 steel wool, maroon synthetic abrasive pad, rags

Buying Materials

For this chest, I used 5/4 poplar, a readily available and inexpensive hardwood. Since poplar this thick isn't always in stock at home centers, this is the time to acquaint yourself with a local hardwood supplier.

If you cannot locate a local lumber dealer, use 1"-thick pine stair tread. The treads should be thick enough to resaw into ⅜"-thick panels. Alternately, you can saw or plane regular ¾"-thick boards, but you'll need to buy and cut twice as much wood since you won't be able to get two boards from each cut.

TOOLS

- Tape measure
- Tablesaw
- Carpenter's handsaw
- Miter saw
- Jigsaw or coping saw
- Sanding drum or dowel
- Drill press (optional)
- 12" combination square
- Block and #4 or #5 handplane
- Card scraper
- Planer (optional)
- Router table
- ¼" straight router bit
- ⅜" straight router bit
- 5/32"-radius by ⅝"-high ogee router bit
- Clamps
- ⅛"drill bit
- ⅜" countersink
- 7/64" centering drill bit
- Drill
- Screwdriver
- Marking knife
- Marking gauge
- ¾" chisel
- Hammer
- Nail set

Building the Blanket Box

You'll need to spend some time preparing your stock before you can begin cutting the joinery. If you're starting with an 8'-long board, you'll first cut the pieces to rough length (about 1" longer than the dimensions given in the materials list), resaw them, plane them, then trim them to the exact dimensions. Use the clearest stock to make the front, top, and sides. You'll also want to use a relatively knot-free section to make the wide bottoms that fit within the box. What's left can be used to make the

WORK SMART

To make this box into a full-size blanket chest, simply double the dimensions given in the materials list. If you intend to store blankets or linens, consider adding an aromatic red cedar liner to the inside of the chest.

apron, false drawer front, and back pieces. Since these pieces are narrower, you can cut around any knots in the wood.

Mill and size your stock

1. Resawing shorter boards is a lot easier than wrestling one 8-footer across the tablesaw. Using a circular saw or miter saw, start by cutting the main pieces of the box from the 5/4 board (see photo A). Cut one piece 20" long for the front and back, one piece 15" long for the sides, and another piece 22" long to make the lid and apron. (If you're already dealing with stock that's ⅜" thick, or are resawing ¾" stock instead of 5/4 material, you'll need

to double the number of boards. If you can't get 9"-wide stock, you may need to double the number of boards and glue them together to make wider panels before proceeding.)

2. Lumber from the mill may not come with a straight edge. If you have a jointer, joint one long edge, then rip the boards so that they are slightly wider than their finished dimensions. If you don't own a jointer, you

A

All you need is one big board. To make things easier to handle, cut the parts to rough length before resawing.

B

Start with a straight edge. The hardboard strip provides a temporary straightedge so that you can safely rip the opposite end with your tablesaw.

Slide the sled, not your stock. **A crosscut sled is an easy and accurate way to cut wide panels. Since it rides on the plywood base, there's no chance of it shifting or tipping at either end of the cut.**

can use your tablesaw, as shown in photo B on p. 39. Make sure your plywood ripping guide has a straight edge, then lay the plywood over the stock you're jointing. With the good edge of the plywood overhanging the edge of the stock, nail the scrap of plywood to

the top of the board with short brad nails. Set the fence so that it just trims the edge of the stock, and guide the plywood against the rip fence.

3. If you're using stock thicker than ⅜", you'll need to resaw or plane the boards down to the proper thickness. To learn how to resaw boards on your tablesaw, see "Skill Builder: Resawing Wood on a Tablesaw" on pp. 42–43. But before you do any resawing, be sure to add a tall auxiliary fence—you'll need to increase the height of your saw's fence in order to safely balance boards on edge (see "Making an Auxiliary Fence" on the facing page).

4. Once the wood is resawn and planed smooth, rip the boards that you've chosen for the sides and bottoms to 7¾". Next, set your saw to 7⅜" and rip one of the bottom boards so that it fits between the back and front. After cutting the boards to width, crosscut both bottom panels to 17⅝" and the sides to 13½". (Crosscutting wide boards isn't a problem if you own a sliding compound miter saw, but if you don't, consider making a sled like the one shown in "Skill Builder: Making a Crosscut Sled," on pp. 44–45).

Shape the boards and cut the joinery

Once the boards are cut to size, you're ready to shape the feet and cut the dadoes and rabbets used to join the case. Take a moment to look at your project before racing through the next two steps. The feet don't need to be a half circle; feel free to change the profile. On a more practical note, you may need to adjust the width of the dadoes for the bottom panels to fit the thickness of your resawn wood.

WORK SMART

Use a roll of masking tape to draw the radius for the side feet. The diameter (even the shape) isn't critical; just make sure the top edge of the foot's profile doesn't intersect with the dado for the bottom panel.

1. Draw the foot profile on the bottom edge of the side pieces (I simply traced the profile

When resawing wide boards or cutting the beveled edge on raised panels at the tablesaw, you'll need to balance boards on their ends and edges. Most fences are too short to safely support the boards during these operations. Attached to your saw's existing fence, an auxiliary fence provides the extra height you'll need to accurately guide the board past the blade.

Not all saw fences are created equal. Some fences have grooves that can accept T-head bolts through the top of the fence. If that's the case with your saw, simply drill a hole in the support board and attach it to the plywood fence. But if your fence has a smooth top, you'll need to rip a spacer strip exactly the same width as the fence so that the auxiliary fence straddles your rip fence snugly, as shown at right.

Different fences call for different designs. A tall auxiliary fence prevents tall boards from tipping, and it can protect the metal fence when the dado cutter is set to make close cuts. Unlike some other jigs, you can keep the fence in place even when making regular rip cuts.

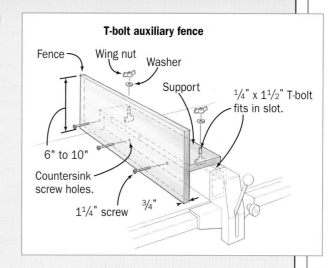

T-bolt auxiliary fence

Fence · Wing nut · Washer · Support · ¼" x 1½" T-bolt fits in slot. · 6" to 10" · Countersink screw holes. · 1¼" screw · ¾"

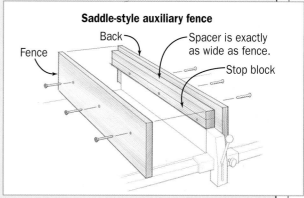

Saddle-style auxiliary fence

Back · Spacer is exactly as wide as fence. · Fence · Stop block

of a roll of tape). Next, cut the profile with a jigsaw or coping saw. To remove marks left by your saw, you can use sandpaper wrapped around a length of dowel as a sanding block or outfit your cordless drill or drill press with a sanding drum (see photo D).

2. Select the best face of each side piece and mark it so that it faces out, then lay out the location of the two ³⁄₁₆"-deep by ⅜"-wide dadoes for the bottom panels. Transfer the lines you just made to the edge of one side piece so that when it's face down on the router table, you can still use it to set the fence. At the router table, set up your router with a ¼"-diameter straight bit and adjust the fence so the bit is between the lines on

D

Drum out the curves. Used in a drill press or chucked into a hand drill, sanding drums quickly smooth curved surfaces. Drilling a hole in the plywood base allows you to use the middle of the drum.

the side piece. If you need to increase the width of your router table in order to cut the upper groove, you can turn the table 90°, as shown in photo E on p. 43. Just remember to feed the stock from right to left, so that the bit's rotation forces the wood against the fence.

What You'll Need

- **Tablesaw with rip blade**
- **Auxiliary fence**
- **⅛"-thick spacer strips**
- **17" to 26" handsaw**
- **Planer or #5 handplane**

A bandsaw is the preferred machine for resawing because it can quickly slice through thick boards without losing a lot of wood to the blade. However, smaller models may not have the horsepower or capacity to handle boards wider than 6". Comparatively, a tablesaw is slower and chews up more wood, but even a small benchtop saw can successfully slice wide boards into thinner stock.

Before resawing, check your stock. A severely bowed or cupped board may be too warped to maneuver safely past the blade. Even if you can manage to resaw warped stock, the final product will require a lot of additional planing to achieve an even thickness.

1. Outfit your tablesaw with an auxiliary fence and a zero-clearance insert with a splitter. (Most saws offer aftermarket inserts that make your tablesaw much safer and are well worth their small price.) Position the fence so that the board is centered on the blade. You may also want to use a featherboard to press the board against the fence as you make the cut.

2. Working alternately from both edges, make a series of shallow cuts, about 1" deep as shown in photo A. Progressively raise the

Slicing two boards from one. Resawing on a tablesaw is slower than with a bandsaw, but with a thin-kerf rip blade, you can slice wide boards easily, even with a smaller saw.

Finish by hand. A handsaw is a safer and more controllable way to finish narrower boards. Insert a wedge in the kerf so the board doesn't pinch the blade.

Plane away the evidence. **Use a bench plane to remove burn or blade marks and get the surface as smooth as possible. If you plane off too much, simply adjust the width of the side dado.**

blade until you reach the maximum cutting depth of the saw. By making the cut in steps, you won't stall your saw, and you'll find that the cut is easier to control.

Note: Don't use your tablesaw to slice all the way through the board. Cutting through the center can cause the feather-board to press the outside slice against the blade, which will cause burn marks and lead to kickback. Use a handsaw to finish the cut.

3. Clamp the board in your bench vise and insert a few spacers in the saw kerf. Using your handsaw, cut through the web of wood left between the kerfs, as shown in photo B.

4. You can expect some blade marks. When power planing, machine all the boards at the same time to ensure that they are all planed to the same thickness. You can also remove the saw marks with a handplane, a scraper, or 100-grit sandpaper (see photo C).

Don't try this with your tablesaw. The router doesn't care if you rotate your table 90° as long as you position the fence behind the bit and feed the stock from right to left.

3. As you did with the bottom and side pieces, cut the boards for the front, false drawer front, skirt, back, and back feet boards to width. Then attach a stop to your crosscut sled to cut the three front pieces and three back boards to 18".

4. To draw a fair curve on the front skirt, make a bow using a thin strip of wood and a piece of string. Use your combination square to establish the beginning, end, and middle of the curve on the board, then adjust the tension of the string until the bow intersects all three points (see photo F). Cut the profile, then sand up to the line.

Draw the bow then draw the curve. **Adjust the string until the center of the bow hits the top of the curve and the outside edges touch the front edges of the feet.**

What You'll Need

- ½" by ¾" by 22" hardwood runners
- ½" by 19" by 24" plywood base
- 1¼" deck screws
- ½" #8 wood screws
- 5/4" by 3½" by 24" wood fence
- 5/4" by 5" by 24" wood fence
- Large drafting triangle or framing square
- Drill with ⅛"-diameter drill and countersink bits
- Small clamps

Crosscutting wide boards on a table-saw—especially if it's a smaller bench-top model—isn't always the most accurate operation. The problem isn't the saw, but the miter gauge. When starting a wide crosscut, the gauge's guide bar may not be far enough into the miter slot to offer sufficient guidance.

This simple fixture is guaranteed to be twice as stable as your miter fence, because it uses both miter slots—and extra-long runners—to line up the cut. Because the entire base slides past the blade, you can use extra clamps to secure your work or add stops for cutting multiple pieces to the same length.

This sled was sized for a benchtop saw, but it will also work for larger machines. Despite its small footprint, it's still capable of crosscutting panels up to 16" wide.

A

Attaching the runners. When drilling the pilot holes through the base for the runners, use a tape flag as an indicator. It can slide up the bit if you don't stop as soon as it touches the plywood.

B

One cut rules them all. Your first cut will be used as the reference line to set the front fence. The back brace holds the base together through the cut.

C

Accuracy is everything. Install one screw, then pivot the fence until it is perfectly perpendicular to the cut line. Install a second screw, then make a few test cuts before installing additional screws.

1. Start by cutting a pair of runners to fit your saw's miter slots. Plane or rip a board on edge so that it slides smoothly in the slot, but without any wiggle. Next, rip two runners from that board that are slightly thinner than the slot's depth.

2. Using your rip fence to position the base, place the plywood on top of your runners. Fasten the base to the runners with glue and ½" wood screws. Mark the drill bit with a piece of tape to ensure that you don't drill through your saw's tabletop (see photo A). Countersink the screw holes so that the heads of the screws don't interfere with your work. Be careful not to countersink so deeply that the screws stick though the bottoms of the runners.

3. Slide the base so that the back edge hangs off the top of the saw. Clamp the back brace flush with the back edge of the base and attach it with glue and 1¼" deck screws. The location of the back brace isn't critical— its job is simply to hold everything together.

4. After attaching the base to the back brace, back up the sled, raise the blade, and make a cut about two-thirds of the way through the base, as shown in photo B.

5. Using the cut as a reference, use a drafting triangle to position the front fence so that it is square to the kerf in the base (see photo C). Take your time when screwing the front fence to the base, because it will be the reference for all future crosscuts. Attach the

A Shopmade Crosscut Sled

With a few careful adjustments, this simple sled can be made to crosscut wide boards as accurately as any expensive aftermarket gauge. Your stock is less likely to shift in midcut because it rests on the plywood instead of sliding across the tablesaw.

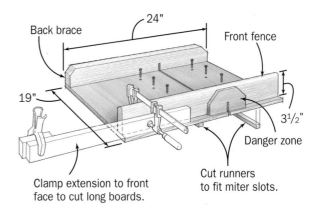

Back brace
24"
Front fence
19"
3½"
Danger zone
Clamp extension to front face to cut long boards.
Cut runners to fit miter slots.

fence about ¾" in from the front edge of the base so that you'll be able to attach extension arms for crosscutting longer boards.

6. Two things to watch out for when using a crosscut sled are cutting through the back brace and/or front fence, and cutting your fingers. The first problem can be avoided by being careful not to raise the blade to full extension. To prevent injuring yourself, attach a scrap of wood to the front fence, as shown in the drawing. Keep your fingers clear of the "danger zone" when making a cut.

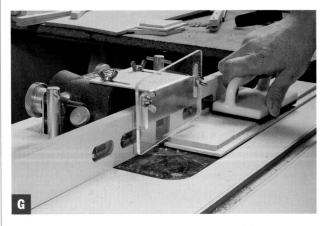

Ship lap, simply done. **Set your router bit to half the width of the back panels, and rabbet opposing edges.**

5. Using a router and a ⅜" straight bit, cut a ⅛"-deep by ⅜"-wide rabbet along the inside-facing ends of the of the front and skirt. Next, without adjusting the router bit or fence, cut the same size rabbet along the bottom edge of the front and the top edge of the skirt.

6. Rather than edge-gluing the three boards to make the back panel, you'll use separate boards with rabbetted edges cut so that each board overlaps the next. The half-lap design provides a closed back but allows the wood to expand and contract to allow for seasonal wood movement. To cut the rabbet, lower the ⅜" straight bit to ³⁄₁₆" high—half the thickness of the wood. Rabbet the ends first (just as you did on the front and skirt), then rout the edges (see photo G).

Router Bits Do Double Duty

Don't let the ball-bearing guide tell you how to use your router bit. You can sometimes get two or three different profiles from a given profile simply by adjusting the cutter height or location of the fence. Here, the bottom half of a Roman ogee substitutes for a ⅛" beading bit.

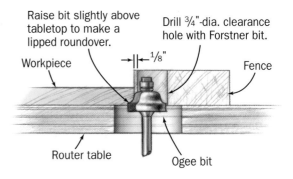

Raise bit slightly above tabletop to make a lipped roundover.

Drill ¾"-dia. clearance hole with Forstner bit.

Workpiece

⟶|⟵ ⅛"

Fence

Router table

Ogee bit

7. Set your miter saw to 30° and then crosscut the back feet to 4¼". Remember to orient the wood so that the long edge has the rabbet.

8. To rout the ¼"-diameter roundover on the skirt, false drawer front, and front pieces, you'll use the bottom half of a standard ⁵⁄₃₂"-radius by ⅝"-high ogee bit. Using your router table, raise the bit so that the roundover section is just above the router table, then position the fence so that only the bottom part of the cutter contacts the wood (see the drawing above).

Assembling the Case

Unlike the bottom panels—which are glued to the sides—the front, skirt, and back boards are simply nailed in place. This is because wood moves along its width at a different rate than its length. If you glued the front to the sides, it might look good for a season or two, but eventually the movement would break the bond. Nails, however, allow for a certain amount of movement and prevent cracking over time. Use a nail set to sink the heads below the surface of the wood, then fill the holes with wood putty.

1. Apply glue to the dadoes you cut in the sides. When you insert the two lower panels, make sure that the narrower one is on top and that both panels are flush with the front edges of the sides. Clamp the sides across the length of the bottom panels, as shown in photo A, then use a tri-square to make sure the assembly is square.

2. The front panel and back pieces were deliberately cut wider than needed, just in case some of your earlier cuts were a little off. Now's the time to trim them to exact width. First, lay the boards in place on the assembled case (you may find it helpful to clamp them in position). As shown in photo B, mark the overhanging lip of the front panel with a pencil and use your tablesaw to trim to the line.

3. Using ⅝" brads, nail the front skirt and panel in place. Start from the feet and work toward the top. When you attach the back boards, place pennies in between the boards to establish a little space for the wood to move, as shown in photo C. Mark and trim the top edge of the upper back board, just as you did with the front panel.

4. Glue blocks are a traditional way to add reinforcement to bottom corners of a box. The

neat thing about corner blocks is that installing them doesn't require clamps. To attach the blocks, simply apply a light coat of glue to the two faces that will contact the skirt and side, then wiggle the block until the glue grabs the wood (see photo D).

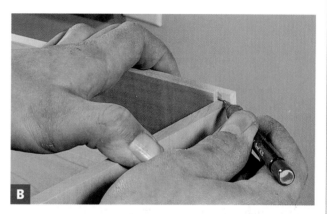

B

Trim to fit. Position the front against the case and use a pencil or knife to mark the exact width.

C

Penny spacer. For big cases, gaps are necessary to allow wood movement; here, they add an interesting detail to the otherwise flat back.

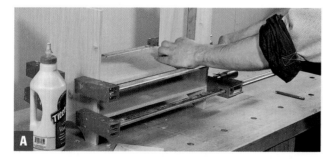

A

Pulling the box together. The bottom panels can be glued to the side because the grain runs in the same direction. Check to see that the assembly is square as you tighten the clamps.

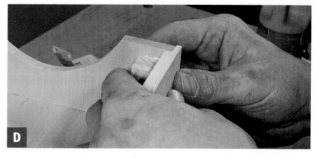

D

Good old glue blocks. Glue blocks reinforce the legs in case of future abuse. Apply glue to adjacent faces of the block, then wiggle it up and down until the glue grabs.

Making the Lid and Adding the Hinges

There's not much to making the lid, but attaching it will give you an opportunity to try your hand at installing mortised hinges. Small jewelry-box-size hinges have leaves that are just 1/16" thick, so you probably won't need a mallet to chop the mortise, but the placement and installation sequence is the same for larger hinges—even those found on entry doors.

1. The materials list states that the dimensions of the lid should be 8⅝" by 19", but check the dimensions of your box first. Size your lid so that it is 1" longer and ½" wider than the dimensions of your box. After cutting the lid to size, cut a ⅛"-deep chamfer along the bottom face of the ends and front edge using a block plane or router.

2. Cleats provide some additional strength to the lid, but their main purpose is to keep the wide panel flat. Without these cross-pieces, odds are good that the lid would resemble a potato chip in a year or two. Cut the cleats to size, then drill and countersink three holes in each, so that the screw heads sit below the surface of the wood. Be careful

Counterbored cleats. One way to use screws that are otherwise too short is to sink the screwheads below the surface. Take care not to bore too deeply, or the screw tips may stick through the top of the lid.

not to countersink too deeply, or the tip of the screw may poke through the top face of the lid (see photo A).

3. Position the cleats on the bottom face of the lid and temporarily clamp them in position. Use a self-centering bit to drill pilot holes in the lid for ¾"-long #4 screws. You can attach the cleats now, but consider removing them before painting the lid. Unpainted, oiled cleats can make an attractive contrast, and they are a nice surprise when you open the box.

Install the hinges

Once the lid is cut to size, you're ready to mortise for hinges on both the box and lid. Woodworking catalogs are packed with all sorts of cup-style and other no-mortise hardware, but you'll find few hinges as versatile as the inexpensive butt hinge. Although most people wouldn't want to tackle a kitchen's worth of cabinetry this way, mortising a few pairs of hinges is an easy

skill to master. You can temporarily install the hinges to make sure that they fit, but remember to remove them before painting.

Start by cutting the mortises and installing the hinges on the lid, then lay out the hinge locations on the back edge of the box. You could do it the other way around, but when attached to the lid, the hinges help balance the lid in place as you secure it to the box.

1. Hold the hinge in place on the lid and score around it using a utility knife. Scoring all the way around three sides of the hinge will keep the wood from splitting as you chisel out wood to flush-mount the hinge (see photo B).

2. To mark out the depth of the mortise, set your marking gauge to the thickness of the leaf, then run the gauge along the back edge of the lid (see photo C).

3. Using the scored markings as a guide, begin chiseling out the mortise. With the chisel's bevel facing down, start by making a line of light chopping cuts (see photo D). Next, with the bevel facing up, pare away the waste (see photo E). Be extra careful not to split the wood around the edges of the mortise.

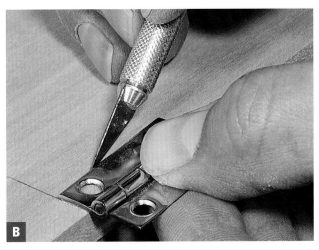

Knifing the line. Using a knife is not only more accurate than a pencil, it also scores the grain, which prevents tearout, and gives you a groove to set your chisel.

Setting your gauge. The mortise should be as deep as the thickness of one leaf. This marking gauge has a cutting wheel that scores the wood just like a knife.

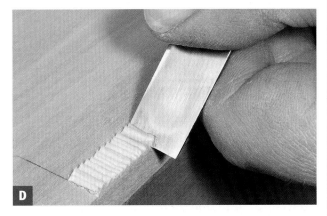

Bevel down and tap lightly. You can use a mallet, but for pine or poplar, you may be able to simply lean into the cut. Don't try to chop all the way down to your line; you'll have more chisel control in the next step.

Bevel up and pare gently. Using your pointer finger to guide the cut, slice off the chips. Start by removing the big chips, then finish up by chiseling to your lines.

If you accidentally make a mortise that's too deep for your hinge, slip a small piece of cardboard or masking tape under the hinge.

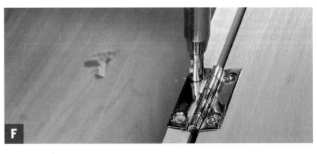

Centering made simple. An ordinary bit will drill holes anywhere but the center of a screw hole. A centering bit's outer sleeve rides against the hinge so the bit stays centered.

4. Once the hinges are installed on the lid, position the lid in place on the box. Again, use a marking knife to score the location of the hinges and a marking gauge to establish the depth of the mortise. If you're using thicker hinges, you may want to start this mortise with a saw, but for thin-leafed hinges, a light tap on your chisel should be plenty (see photo F).

5. Once the wood is chiseled out, predrill the holes for the mounting screws that will hold the hinge in place. To ensure that the holes are centered precisely, you may want to use a self-centering bit. The sleeve centers the bit on the hole in the hinge.

Building the Drawer

The drawer for this box is similar to that of the desk organizer except that the bottom is "raised," or beveled, along the ends and front edge. The bevel reduces the thickness of the ³⁄₈"-thick panel so it fits into the ¼"-wide groove. Raised panels are commonly used for drawer bottoms, door panels, and other frame-and-panel assemblies.

1. Use the dimensions given in the materials list as a guide, but remember to cut the drawer front and side pieces so that they slide between the two wood panels. It doesn't matter if the size varies a little from the materials list, just make sure the fit is smooth in the case.

2. Next, use your tablesaw or router table to cut a ¼"-wide by ³⁄₁₆"-deep groove (to house the drawer bottom) along the bottom edges of the front and side pieces. Rather than

Sled-cut sides. The sides of the drawer are too short to cut safely with a miter gauge. Add stops to both sides of the sled's fence so that the rabbets can be accurately nibbled away by the rip blade.

switching to a dado blade, you can cut the groove by making a few passes with your regular sawblade. Similarly, you can attach a pair of stops to the front fence of your crosscut sled, as shown, to make the dadoes on the sides for the back of the drawer (see

B

A beveled bottom. A tall auxiliary fence provides extra support when beveling the bottom of the drawer. The width of the bevel can vary with the angle of the blade. Sneak up on the cut so that you don't remove too much on the first pass.

photo A). (If you didn't make the crosscut sled, you can also use a miter gauge to guide the sides past the blade.)

3. Once you've cut the bottom to 7¼" by 16¾", you're ready to cut the bevel on the tablesaw. Set your saw to cut a 12° bevel, but realize that the actual angle isn't critical.

The object is to establish a bevel that allows the edge of the drawer bottom to fit snugly within the groove—too snug is better than too loose at this point (see photo B). If the bevel is a tad tight, use a block plane to sneak up on a perfect fit (see photo C).

4. Glue the drawer front and back to the sides, clamp the assembly together, and check to see that the drawer is square.

5. Next, slide the bottom in the groove, locate the position of the screw, and drill a pilot hole. Because it is a solid wood panel, the bottom must also be able to move. To allow for this, cut a thin notch from the pilot hole to the bottom's back edge (see photo D).

6. Attach the false front to the drawer using yellow glue and a few clamps, then drill the holes in the front of the drawer for the two 1"-diameter knobs. Use your combination square to position the holes 1⅜" up from the bottom and 3½" in from the sides, as shown in the drawing on p. 37. Size the holes one bit size larger than the screws holding the knobs so that the threads don't bite into the drawer front.

C

Planed to perfection. If sawing wood on edge starts to feels dicey, use a block plane. A few swipes might be all you need to remove saw marks and slide the bottom into the side grooves.

D

Screw instead of glue. Unlike plywood bottoms, this panel needs room to move. The screw sits in a slot, allowing the wood to expand and contract with seasonal changes in humidity.

Finishing the Box

Poplar is inexpensive and easy to work with hand tools, but few admire the green tinge of the wood. Milk paint is a great way to add a little color while keeping with the country style of this box. A relatively simple mix of lime, casein (milk protein), clay, and pigment, milk paint is different than regular latex or oil paints because it does not chip or peel, but wears away to reveal wood or additional colors beneath. Woodworkers used to mix their own, but today, milk paint is available in 16 premixed colors. All you have to do is add water (see Sources on p. 170).

Milk paint isn't perfect. Because it contains no preservatives, the paint can spoil, just like regular milk. For that reason, mix only as much as you need. You can extend the working time of mixed paint for a few days by storing it in the refrigerator, but if it starts to smell, pour it down the drain and mix up a fresh batch. Since milk paint tends to stain easily, you'll need to protect it with a top coat of varnish or boiled linseed oil.

1. Like other water-based finishes, milk paint will raise the grain of the wood. To prevent this, first sand the surface with 150-grit sandpaper, then wipe it down with a damp sponge. After the wood is dry, knock off the raised fibers (also called "whiskers") with 220-grit sandpaper. Be careful not to sand too much, or you may cut into the surface of the wood, which will only lead to more whiskers when you apply the paint.

2. Because it's such a thin-bodied paint, even the smallest imperfection in the wood will stand out. Fill all dents, nail holes, even

> **WORK SMART**
>
> Planing produces a finished surface that won't whisker like sanding because it slices, rather than scratches, the surface. Don't worry about plane marks. Minor ripples or tracks will add an extra tactile quality under the milk-paint finish.

pinhead-size knots with latex filler. Slightly overfill the holes, then level the patches with 220-grit sandpaper when dry.

3. To mix the paint, start by using equal amounts of water and dry mix, then add more water—a few drops at a time—until you get a mix that's smooth enough to spread, but still thick enough to cover the wood. Give the jar a good shake so that it's well mixed, then allow the mixed paint to sit for about 30 minutes. Pour the paint through cheesecloth to strain out any large particles, as shown in photo A.

Shaken, stirred, and strained. You can expect a few chunks of unmixed milk paint. Strain the paint through cheesecloth to produce a smooth consistency.

Just brush it on. The water in the milk paint is immediately absorbed by the wood. Don't worry about brush marks, just lay it on as evenly as possible.

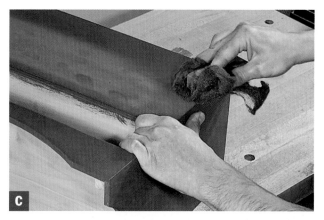

Burnish to a glow. Dry milk paint is hard enough to polish. Start with a maroon abrasive pad, then move up to 000 steel wool.

4. Lay on the first coat using a combination of dabbing and brushing strokes (see photo B). Don't worry if it doesn't look even at this point; the goal is simply to avoid leaving any drips or puddles on the wood. As you apply it, stir the paint to keep the solids from settling. The first coat will dry to the touch in minutes, but you'll want to wait at least 4 hours between coats. Once it's dry, the first coat will look blotchy, but don't worry. The paint will start to show its true colors by the second coat.

5. After applying two or three coats of paint, rub down every square inch of your project with a maroon (medium-grit) abrasive pad until the paint turns chalky white. At that point, switch over to 000 steel wool and continue rubbing until the paint develops a shiny, burnished look (see photo C).

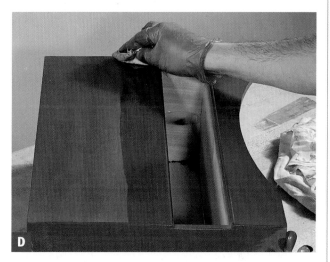

Oil brings out the color. Use either boiled linseed oil or a wipe-on varnish to seal the surface and bring out milk paint's rich color.

6. Protect your finish with a coat of wipe-on varnish or boiled linseed oil (see photo D). Apply the oil with a rag, wait 10 minutes, then wipe off any excess finish. Apply the same finish to the knobs and cleats.

7. After the oil has dried, reattach the cleats to the bottom of the lid, and the hinges holding the lid to the box. The knobs for the drawer should thread easily onto the machine screws. For added sheen, you can add a coat of paste wax to the outside of the blanket box.

WORK SAFE

Curing linseed oil generates enough heat to spontaneously combust. To avoid the risk of fire, hang oily rags outdoors until they are thoroughly dry. When the finish is fully cured, the rags can be discarded with regular trash.

Storage Bench

The Arts and Crafts movement, which flourished in Europe and America from 1870 to 1920, is often noted for a few simple tenets—honesty of materials, solidity of construction, utility, adaptability to place, and aesthetic effect—all of which can be seen in this storage bench. The bench's straight lines and solid joinery make a strong statement, but adding a couple of seat cushions (available at any home store) transforms it into a soft, comfortable seat. In addition, the top is hinged so you can use the bench to hide boots, blankets, or any other items that pile up next to the back door or at the foot of the bed.

Building projects like this, instead of ordering them from a catalog or fighting for them at an auction, is very much in keeping with the spirit of the piece. The father of the American Arts and Crafts movement, Gustav Stickley, is best known as a furniture maker, but he also published a popular magazine called *The Craftsman,* which aired the philosophy of the movement and was one of the first do-it-yourself magazines. Working in basement and garage workshops, passionate amateurs used plans published in the magazine just as you are using this book today. (By the way, *Mission* is used interchangeably with *Craftsman*, but the term infuriated Stickley, as it was used by one of his competitors.)

If you visit an antique store, you may observe collectors crawling under tables and chairs as they search for a sticker bearing the Stickley motto: *Als ik kan* (As best I can). But you don't need to buy a $500,000 sideboard to appreciate the value of those three words. The pleasure you feel from working in your shop and the skills you learn when making something yourself is really what it's all about.

What You'll Learn

- **Making four-sided quartersawn legs**
- **Using a biscuit jointer**
- **Using a slot-cutting router bit**
- **Cutting tenons with a dado cutter**
- **Keeping panels square during assembly**

Keep assemblies square. This simple assembly table ensures perfect glue-ups.

Arts and Crafts furniture is distinguished by strong (almost exaggerated) joinery, such as large tenons sticking through even thicker legs. As you learn additional woodworking skills, you may elect to follow Stickley's instructions to the letter, but there are easier ways to get the same effect. Building this storage bench, you'll learn to use a biscuit jointer to quickly connect the rails to the legs. This tool cuts a small slot in both mating pieces, then employs a wooden disk (the biscuit), which works like a small tenon to connect the two pieces. You'll still get a chance to cut a few tenons as you make the stiles, the vertical pieces of wood that fit between the horizontal rails.

Since the bench is composed of many identical pieces and symmetrical assemblies, this project enables you to think about how projects "flow" through your shop. To mini-

Cutting slots with a router. Your router is good for more than shaping edges. You'll learn to use a slot cutter to make frame-and-panel assemblies, which can be used for making doors and cabinets of any size.

Nibbling tenons. Many woodworkers cut tenons with a tablesaw and dado cutter. Here, you'll get to try that technique on for size.

A Step Beyond Your Basic Bench

Frame-and-panel construction enables you to build big pieces in a small space. Plywood panels save time and expense without compromising good looks.

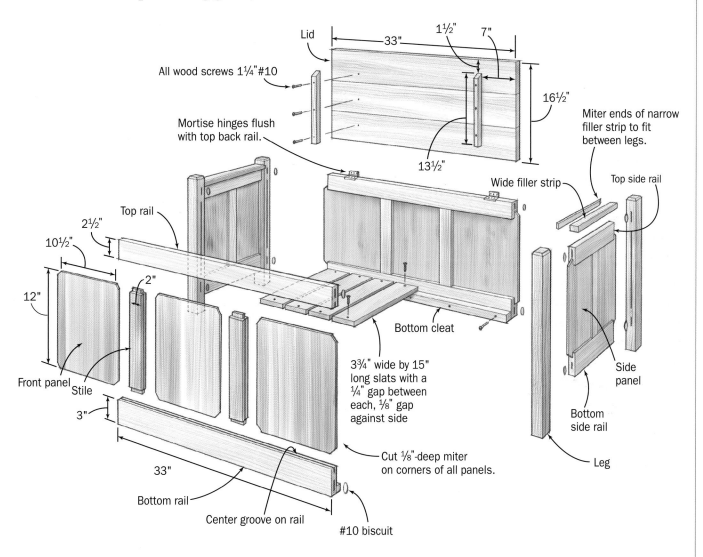

Lid

All wood screws 1¼" #10

Mortise hinges flush with top back rail.

33" 1½" 7"

16½"

13½"

Miter ends of narrow filler strip to fit between legs.

Wide filler strip

Top side rail

Top rail

2½"

10½"

12"

2"

Front panel Stile

3"

33"

Bottom rail

Center groove on rail

Bottom cleat

3¾" wide by 15" long slats with a ¼" gap between each, ⅛" gap against side

Cut ⅛"-deep miter on corners of all panels.

#10 biscuit

Side panel

Bottom side rail

Leg

---

mize measurement-related errors, prepare your stock so that you set your miter saw or tablesaw once, then cut all the pieces that are the same size at one time. To ensure that same-size panels turn out that way, and a groove cut along one board aligns with its mate, you'll learn how to use spacer boards

and jigs that eliminate the need for a tape measure. You'll also learn how to make and use an assembly table that not only frees up space on your bench, but also squares up assemblies so that you can concentrate on clamping before the glue sets.

MATERIALS STORAGE BENCH

Quantity	Part	Actual Size	Notes
8	Leg cores	¾" x 1" x 22½"	Quartersawn white oak is preferred throughout this list, but any hardwood will work. Cut the legs long and trim to length after attaching the veneer.
8	Leg veneers	¼" x 1½" x 22½"	Start with 2"-wide strips. Trim to final width after gluing to sides of leg core.
2	Top side rails	¾" x 2½" x 14"	
2	Bottom side rails	¾" x 3" x 14"	
2	Top front and back rails	¾" x 2½" x 33"	
2	Bottom front and back rails	¾" x 3" x 33"	
6	Stiles	¾" x 2" x 12"	
4	Side panels	¼" x 6½" x 12"	You can cut 10 panels (plus a few extra) from a half sheet of ¼" oak plywood.
6	Front and back panels	¼" x 10½" x 12"	
1	Lid	¾" x 16½" x 33"	
2	Lid cleats	¾" x 1" x 13½"	
2	Wide filler strips	¾" x 1" x 14"	
2	Narrow filler strips	¾" x ¼" x 14½"	Cut 1" longer than needed. Miter the ends to fit between the legs after assembling the bench.
2	Bottom cleats	¾" x 1" x 33"	
8	Bottom slats	¾" x 2½" x 15"	Pine or poplar is fine. Your boots won't know the difference.
12	#10 Biscuits		Buy a container.
2	No-mortise hinges	3" x ¾"	See Sources on p. 170.
16	1¼" #10 wood screws		
	Polyurethane glue		For laminating legs
	Yellow glue		For gluing biscuits and panels
	150-grit and 220-grit sandpaper		You'll need packs of both sheets and disks.
1 pint	Watco® oil		Dark walnut
2 cans	Spray polyurethane		Satin finish
	Respirator		For use when spraying.

Buying Materials

Although many different types of wood were used during the Arts and Crafts period, quartersawn white oak was the wood of choice. Quartersawing produces lumber that is less prone to warping, which is in keeping with two of the movement's guiding principles: strength and permanence. An important side benefit is that quartersawing white oak also reveals a handsome ray fleck figure. You can find quartersawn white oak at most local mills, and for a small extra fee they'll mill it to the ¾" thickness

TOOLS

- Tape measure
- Tablesaw with a good rip blade
- Miter saw
- Biscuit jointer
- 12" combination square
- Block and #4 or #5 handplane
- Card scraper
- Bearing-guided chamfer bit
- Router
- ½"-diameter by 1"-high flush-trimming router bit
- ¼"-wide by ¼"-deep slot-cutting router bit
- Clamps
- ⅛"-diameter drill bit
- ⅜" countersink bit
- Drill
- Screwdriver

you'll need for this project. If white oak is unavailable or prohibitively expensive, consider substituting red oak.

Building the Bench

This is a larger project than those in earlier chapters, but it's not difficult to build—even if your shop is a cramped corner of your garage or basement. This bench breaks down into three bite-size subassemblies: the legs, the panels, and the top. Plan on spending a day to cut and assemble each section and a few hours the following weekend to pull the bench together and apply a finish.

As you build each section, pay close attention to the grain. The fleck pattern on the legs is sure to run in a different direction than the rails, but try to arrange the wood so that the fronts of both front legs match and the top rails complement the bottoms. You'll appreciate the difference this detail makes as soon as you wipe on the first coat of stain.

Making the Legs

The ray-flecked grain of quartersawn wood is a signature of Arts and Crafts furniture. The problem with using a solid leg is that the flecks will only appear on two opposite sides (and one of those sides will be hidden by joinery). There are several solutions, such as mitering the edges of four boards or using a fancy lock-miter bit on your router table. But the simplest fix, described here, is to make the leg slightly undersize in thickness and then glue quartersawn strips to the two straight-grained sides. The glue line between the thin veneer and leg blank will disappear after you chamfer the edges.

1. Glue up the core portion of the legs first. Start by ripping two 4"-long boards to 2½" wide. Arrange the boards so that the best fleck figure faces out. Wipe a thin coat of polyurethane glue onto the inside face of one board and clamp the other on top. Once the glue has cured, knock off the dried foam with a scraper. Joint one edge (a #4 or #5 handplane works fine), then rip two 1"-wide lengths. Using your miter saw, cut the lengths in half to make four 24"-long core pieces.

Leg Detail

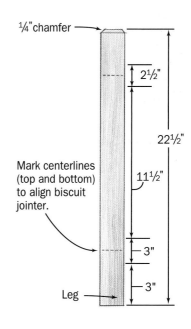

¼" chamfer

2½"

22½"

11½"

Mark centerlines (top and bottom) to align biscuit jointer.

3"

3"

Leg

2. To make the ¼" veneers that hide the core's glue line, you'll need to resaw a ¾" by 4" by 48" board. (For more on this process, see "Skill Builder: Resawing Wood on a Tablesaw" on pp. 42–43. Set your rip fence just a hair thicker than ¼" so that you'll be able to remove saw marks or burns with a handplane. After resawing, crosscut the veneers to

24" and attach them to the core pieces with polyurethane glue. As you tighten the clamps, make sure that the veneers slightly protrude over both edges.

3. The veneers were cut wider than the core to allow for slippage during glue-up. Once the glue has dried, trim them flush with a router and flush-trimming bit (a bearing-driven straight bit). Knock excess glue off the leg, if necessary, then set the bit so that the bearing rides against the center of the leg (see photo A). Remember to feed the stock from right to left, against the rotation of the bit.

4. Using the router table and a 45° bearing-driven chamfer bit, raise the bit so that the top edge of the chamfer just touches the glue line, then rout all four edges of each leg (see photo B). When finished, the glue line will be unseen because it's aligned with the edge of the chamfer.

5. Trim the four legs to 22½" long at the miter saw. Next, set the saw to cut a 45° bevel and cut a ¼"-tall chamfer on the top ends of all four legs. To make an even chamfer on all four sides, clamp a stop block to your saw's fence so all you need to do is rotate the leg and make the cut.

6. The best way to avoid measurement-related layout mistakes is to mark out the locations of the top and bottom rails on all four legs at once. Position the bottoms of the legs against a straightedge, such as your framing square, and use your combination square as shown in photo C on the facing page. Mark the locations of the top and bottom edges of the rails, then mark the center-lines for both rails. You'll use these reference lines to cut the biscuit slots.

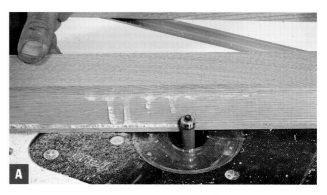

A

Flush-cut edges. Position the bit's bearing against the core.

B

Chamfering the edges. Set the chamfer bit to the height of the veneer. Chamfering hides the glue joint and softens sharp oak corners.

Wraparound Quartersawn Legs

To make square legs—even if your wood isn't exactly as thick as the dimensions in the drawing—adjust the width of the core so that it's equal to the leg thickness minus twice the thickness of the veneer.

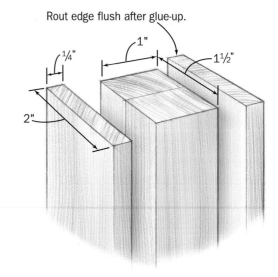

How a board is cut from a log can make a big difference in the appearance of the wood. Most boards are flatsawn—the log is sliced tangentially to the annual growth rings—a method that produces an arched or "cathedral" grain pattern on the faces. Flatsawing is fast and produces the most usable wood from a given log, but flatsawn boards have a tendency to cup. In some projects, like this one, the arched grain can be distracting unless carefully arranged.

Quartersawn boards are cut so that the annual rings are perpendicular to the face of the board. Quartersawing involves more work (the log is first cut into quarters and reoriented before every cut so that the blade is perpendicular to the annual rings) and produces narrower boards than flatsawing, but the straight-grained stock is stronger and less likely to warp. In some species (oak especially), it also produces large cross-grain flecks, which are a favorite with builders of Arts and Crafts furniture.

The quartersawing process doesn't always produce boards with rings perpendicular to the face. When the annual rings run from 30° to 60° to the face of the wood, it's considered riftsawn. Riftsawn boards are straight grained and are more dimensionally stable than flatsawn, but most of them lack the bold fleck figure found on true quartersawn stock.

7. The rails are offset from the inside edges of the legs by ¼". The simplest way to cut matching biscuit slots is to use a ¼"-thick spacer instead of the biscuit jointer's fence to slot the legs. Using your benchtop as the reference surface, position the leg so that the inside face is against your workbench. Place the biscuit jointer on top of the spacer, then align the centering mark on the biscuit jointer with the centerline on the leg, and cut the slot for the top rail as shown in photo D below. After cutting the slot for the bottom rail, flip the leg end over end so that the inside face of the leg is facedown on the bench before cutting the slots for the adjacent corner.

C

Measure once, then mark all four at once. When marked off in one swipe, the legs won't be off even the width of a pencil line.

D

Biscuit the legs. To create a ¼" offset, position the leg so the outside face is against the benchtop and insert a hardboard spacer beneath your biscuit jointer as shown.

Building the Sides

The next steps cover the assembly process for the two side panels. But at the same time, you will also cut many of the pieces you'll need to build the front and back panels. Making all the same-size cuts at once saves time and reduces errors.

1. Set your tablesaw fence to 3" and rip enough wood to make two 14"-long bottom side rails and two 33"-long bottom front and bottom rear rails. Reset the fence to 2½" and cut the four matching top rails. Next, set the fence to 2" and rip enough wood for the six 12½"-long stiles that will be used for the side, front, and back assemblies. Using your miter saw or crosscut sled, cut the rails and stiles to final length.

2. Cut the plywood panels next. Set your rip fence to 12". Orient the half sheet of ¼"-thick plywood so that the grain on the good (top) face is running perpendicular to the blade and cut three strips.

3. Use the crosscut sled to cut four 6½"-wide panels for the sides and six 10½"-wide panels

for the front and back. You may want to cut a few extra panels with the leftover wood just in case you notice an ugly glue line in the veneer or mismatched grain later on. To allow for the radius left in the inside corners by the slot cutter router bit, set your miter saw to 45° and nip ⅛" off the corners of the panels.

4. Take a close look at your rail pieces and mark the face with the least attractive grain as the back. Next, lay the back face of the rail against your bench, mark the centerline, and use your biscuit jointer to cut slots in both ends (see photo A). (The slot won't be centered exactly on the thickness of your stock. Using a spacer to raise the slot on the leg and no spacer when slotting the rails automatically establishes a stepped or offset joint.)

5. With the back face of the side assembly facing up, dry-assemble the side rails to the legs. (Because biscuits are designed to allow some "wiggle room," it's easy to accidentally assemble a panel out of square. To prevent this, use the self-squaring assembly table shown in photo B.)

A

Biscuit the rails. Lay the "good" face of the rail against your bench and cut a slot without a spacer. By doing this, the biscuit connecting it to the leg will automatically establish the ¼" offset.

B

Measurements not required. Cutting two spacers from scrap to establish the height of the legs and panel height is faster and just as accurate as using a tape measure and triangle.

What You'll Need

- ■ ¾" by 4' by 4' plywood
- ■ ¾" by 3" by 2' wood or wood strips
- ■ Two sawhorses
- ■ Framing square
- ■ Drill with bits and driver
- ■ 1¼" deck screws
- ■ Foam brush
- ■ Polyurethane
- ■ Wax

This fixture is about as simple as it gets—all it takes is a half sheet of plywood or particleboard, a few scraps of wood, and a pair of sawhorses—but once built, it's likely to become a permanent fixture in your shop. The two built-in squaring strips serve as a reliable reference point when assembling doors or panels. Simply position one side of your project against one strip, then clamp the other against the second strip to establish a square corner. The squaring guide is useful when assembling doors, the side panels of this bench, or any square assembly, but for those times when you need a smooth, flat surface, just flip the top.

1. Start with a half sheet of ¾"-thick plywood or particleboard. Apply two to three coats of polyurethane, making sure to thoroughly seal the ends.

2. Using a framing square as a guide, attach two strips of wood in an L-form with 1¼" deck screws. If you plan to build doors, leave a gap along the inside corner so that the rails can stick through, as shown. (Consider these guides sacrificial; you trim them as needed to fit a clamp or work around a protruding tenon.)

3. Apply a heavy coat of paste wax to the top and the guides. Apply another coat of wax whenever it takes more than a light pass with a scraper to pop off dried paint or glue.

A Self-Guided Assembly Table

Screwing a pair of guide strips to your assembly table ensures that at least one corner of your glue-up is square. It's especially useful when building frame-and-panel assemblies

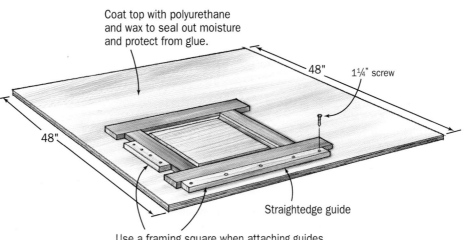

Coat top with polyurethane and wax to seal out moisture and protect from glue.

48"

1¼" screw

48"

Straightedge guide

Use a framing square when attaching guides to ensure that they are square to each other. Trim guides as needed to work around glue-ups.

Cut grooves to accept the panels

Since this may be your first frame-and-panel case piece, the joinery process is designed to enable you to see how everything goes together even before you finish cutting all the parts. You'll dry-assemble the (panel-less) sides of the case, then use your router and slot-cutting bit to groove the panels and stiles. Cutting the slot this way prevents the chance of accidentally grooving the wrong edge, stops the slot cutter from cutting all the way down the leg, and ensures that the grooves line up on all four sides. Just as you did when cutting the biscuit slots, you'll use spacers throughout the process to ensure accurate alignment—without having to adjust the depth of your router or even use a ruler.

1. Dry-assemble one side of the bench so that the outside (good) face is against your benchtop. You'll notice that the inside face of the rails are offset from the legs by ¼". To provide a level surface for your router, temporarily attach two ¼"-thick hardboard spacers to the rails with carpet tape.

2. A ¼"-wide by ¼"-deep slot-cutting bit is basically a miniature sawblade. Grooving

with a router, instead of your tablesaw, enables you to cut the panel grooves in the legs and rails in one step. Adjust the height of the bit so that the slot is roughly centered on the edge of the rail. Rest the base of the router on the side assembly and feed it around the inside of the frame in a clockwise direction (see photo C). Repeat the same process on the other side panel.

3. After routing the grooves for the two side panels, the next step is to groove the legs for the front and back panels. To do this, use your side rails as shorter "stand-ins." Disassemble the side panels and rotate the legs so that the short (side) rails are positioned where the longer (front and back) rails will be and clamp them in place. Remember that the back faces of the legs and rails are still facing up. Attach

Simply slotting. Center the slot cutter on the middle of the rail, then slot the side and leg to accept the plywood panel. Attach hardboard strips to the leg to compensate for the offset.

Routing long rails. It's easier to rout the long rails on your bench. Position the piece so the good side faces up, clamp a ¼"-thick hardboard spacer, then rout the slot from left to right.

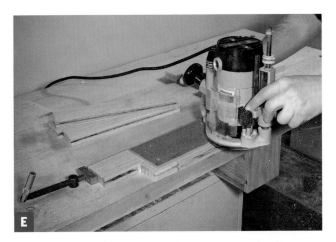

Stile-slotting jig. This simple setup keeps clamps out of your way so that you can slot the stiles in one pass.

Dado-cutting short tenons. Nibble out a ¼"-long stub tenon on both ends of the stiles. Use the groove you routed in the edges as a guide.

the ¼"-thick hardboard spacers to the rails and rout the legs, just as before.

4. To rout panel grooves in the front and back rails, position the boards on your bench with the good faces down. Again, use a ¼"-thick hardboard spacer between the router and rail as you rout the groove, as shown in photo D, on p. 64. You will need to stop the router and reposition your clamps in order to finish cutting the groove.

5. The edges of the stiles must also be grooved to accept the panels. Short pieces can be tough to clamp, so you may want to build a grooving jig, like the one shown in the drawing at right. Position the stile in the jig so that the back face is oriented up. As you rout the groove (see photo E), remember to run the router from left to right, against the rotation of the bit.

6. The end of each stile has a small tenon that fits into the grooved rails just like the plywood panels. To cut this tenon, replace your tablesaw's blade with a ½"-wide dado cutter. Adjust the cutter's height so that it comes up just to the height of the groove.

Stile-Grooving Jig

Made from scraps of plywood, this simple jig will hold the stiles in place as you rout the grooves.

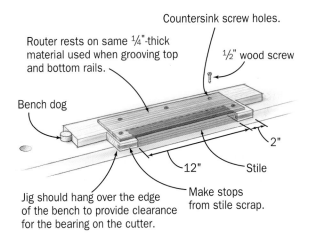

Countersink screw holes.

Router rests on same ¼"-thick material used when grooving top and bottom rails.

½" wood screw

Bench dog

2"

12"

Stile

Jig should hang over the edge of the bench to provide clearance for the bearing on the cutter.

Make stops from stile scrap.

Next, slide the rip fence so that it's ½" away from the inside edge of the cutter. Use your saw's miter gauge to guide the stile as you make the cut (see photo F). In the event that your slot isn't perfectly centered on the stile, cut the tenon on the front or back face of all the stiles, test the fit, then double-check the height of the cutter before cutting the opposite faces.

Assembling the Box

To reduce the number of clamps needed, and to eliminate the insanity of a complex glue-up, this bench is glued together in steps: The sides are assembled first, then the front and back, and then the box is joined together. With time on your side, check each subassembly carefully to make sure that everything stays square as it's clamped together. During this process, you'll learn techniques to keep the pieces perpendicular so you can focus on juggling clamps and wiping away glue drips with a damp rag before they dry into hard, unstainable lumps.

1. Start with the side panels. Position the legs, panels, and short rails on your assembly table so that the good sides face up. Install biscuits and glue, use the 3"-wide spacer to set the height of the bottom rail, then insert the panel and stile. Once pieces are assembled and clamped together, use a drafting triangle to double-check that everything is square (see photo A). If not, reposition the clamps to make adjustments.

2. Assemble the front and back panels next. To align the ends of the top and bottom rails, you'll need to make a pair of grooved clamp boards. The clamp boards will take the place of the legs during this step of glue-up. Start-

A

Pulling it all together. Pay attention to the distance between the outside edges of the rails to the ends of the legs. The biscuits may slide a little as you tighten the clamps.

B

Grooved clamping caul. Cutting a ½"-deep groove on the cauls allows you to align the ends of the rails and establishes the length of the plywood tongue.

These simple braces help keep the overall assembly square as you pull everything together at glue-up. They can be made simply by mitering the corners off any scrap of ¾"-thick plywood or MDF. (Factory-cut edges are about as square as they come, but if you're not sure if you or the factory made the cut, check the outside corner with a drafting triangle or framing square to be sure.) Drill holes through the outside corners so that you can use them to hold your clamps. You may also want to nip the inside corner so that it doesn't get in the way of (or accidentally become glued to) the pieces you glue together.

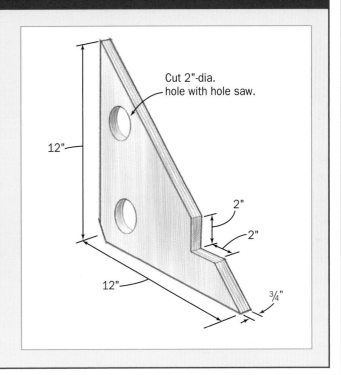

Cut 2"-dia. hole with hole saw.

12"

2"

2"

12"

¾"

ing with two pieces of ¾"-thick by 16"-long scrap, rout a ¼"-wide by ¼"-deep groove along one edge (see photo B). The plywood should fit into the groove, enabling you to butt the ends of both rails against the edge of the caul (see photo B inset) wood.

3. Once the glue has cured, carefully inspect the front and side panels for glue stains, black stains (left by pipe clamps), or uneven spots where the rails meet the stiles. Sand, scrape, or plane away these imperfections, as shown in photo C at right, then finish-sand the legs and rails up through 220 grit.

4. It's finally time to assemble your bench. Position a side assembly so that the inside face is up. Insert two scrap 2x4s under the side to provide clearance for the clamps. As you glue and clamp the front panel in place, use a 3"-wide (leg) spacer to make sure that the lower rails of all four sides are the same distance from the bottom of the leg. As you

remove the clamps to attach the back panel, keep a plywood triangle in place for support (see photo D on p. 68).

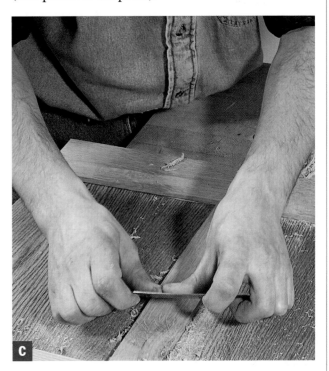

C

Scrape the stiles. A scraper is useful for removing glue drips and flattening any ledge that might exist between the stiles and rails.

Triangles serve as an extra pair of hands. The squaring jigs prevent the back from tipping as you tighten the panel clamps. They also ensure that corners stay square as the glue dries.

Clamp up the case. Insert wood spacers under the bench to allow clearance for the clamps. Positioning triangles in opposite corners helps keep things square.

5. Now that both sides are glued into one side panel, you'll need to glue the front and back to the remaining side in one step. Use the squaring braces to ensure that the bench

stays square as you tighten the clamps (see photo E). If opposing corners line up with the plywood triangles, you can be certain that the case is square.

Finish out the inside

1. To secure the bottom of the bench, you'll use two cleats attached to the insides of the front and back assemblies. Cut the two bottom cleats to size, then drill and countersink the holes needed to screw them to the front and back bottom rails, as shown in photo F on the facing page.

2. Double-check the inside dimension of the box before cutting the bottom slats to size. Before installing the slats, chamfer the top edges with either a router or a handplane. Next, position the slats on the bottom cleats inside the bench. There should be a ¼" gap between the boards. Exact spacing is not

> **WORK SMART**
>
> **W**hen attaching the slats, start at both ends and work toward the center. If your spacing is a little off, try adjusting the spacing between boards or planing off a small amount from a few of the center boards.

critical, but make sure the gap looks even before you screw the boards in place (see photo G).

3. The lid sits between the legs. To conceal the edge of the top rails, I used filler strips cut to fit between the legs. The 1¼"-wide

A cleat to hold on to. Screw a pair of cleats to the bottom edge of the lower front and back rails. Use clamps to hold the cleat flush to the bottom edge as you screw it in place.

Plank by plank. As you install the planked bottom, start from the outside ends and work inward.

filler strip looks like a single piece of wood, but it's made up of two strips, a wider piece that fits between the flat portion of the legs, and a narrow piece that's mitered to fit between the chamfers cut on the inside corners (see photo H). Start by making two 2¾"-wide by 15"-long strips (one for each side of the top). Rip a ¾" strip off both boards. Next cut the two wider boards so that they fit between the front and back legs. Rip the boards so that the edges of the wide filler boards touch the inside edges of the chamfers on the legs.

Two strips are easier than one. Cut the square and miter end from two different strips, then glue them together.

4. Set your miter saw to 45° and miter one end of the thinner filler strip. Placing it against the wider strip you just made, butt the mitered end against one chamfer and mark the opposite end, as shown in photo I. Miter the opposite end, then glue the two pieces together. The filler strip assembly is then simply glued to the top edge of the side rail.

Miter reminder. Use a thick pencil line as a reminder not to flip the strip the wrong way when you bring it to the saw. Mark the actual cut with a knife or sharp pencil.

Making the Lid

When building a wide panel, as for a tabletop or lid, spelling out exact dimensions of each board doesn't work well in the real world. You will need to look at your wood as you refer to the materials list. Depending on what's available, you may be able to assemble the top from two boards, or you may need three or more. If you pay attention to the grain and strive for tight-fitting glue lines, either choice can be equally attractive.

1. Edge-join as many boards as necessary to make a panel that is slightly larger than the final 16½" x 33" lid. Trim the lid to the final dimensions after glue-up. (If the lid is too wide for your crosscut sled, you may need to cut it with a circular saw. To learn how to use a circular saw to cut square edges on wide panels, see "Skill Builder: Making an Edge Cutting Guide" on p. 77.

2. Cut the two lid cleats to size, then drill and countersink the screw holes used to attach the cleats to the lid. The holes on the far ends of each cleat should be wider to allow the screw to pivot as the lid moves with seasonal changes in humidity. To make these elongated holes, flip the board so that the cleat is facing lid edge up, and drill a ⅝"-diameter hole up to the countersunk hole you made on the opposite edge. Next, redrill the pilot hole, but tilt the drill to elongate the center of the hole as shown in photo A.

3. Place the lid facedown on your bench and attach the cleats with six 1¼" screws.

4. The two leaves of a no-mortise hinge are designed to fold into each other, minimizing but not completely eliminating the thickness of the metal hinge. To make the lid sit flush, the hinge should be mortised into the top rail. Position the hinge on the rail and use a marking knife to lay out your mortise lines (see photo B). Next, use a marking gauge, set to the thickness of the hinge, to establish the depth of the mortise. Make a series of shallow cuts with a dovetail saw, then use a chisel to pare out the waste.

Room to grow. Screwing the cleats to the lid prevents the panel from cupping, but widening the outer cleat holes allows the lid to move with seasonal changes in humidity.

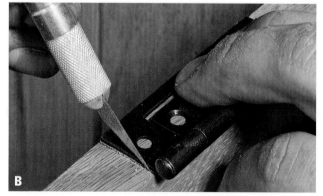

Mortise the upper back rail. Mark their location with a utility knife, then chisel out each mortise by hand.

Finishing

The best way to get the plywood panels to match the solid wood rails and stiles is to use a dark stain. A pigmented oil varnish can be used as a finish by itself, but you'll probably want the extra stain and scuff protection offered by a polyurethane varnish. As a side benefit, alkyd-based polyurethanes add a slight amber tint to the wood, which more closely resembles the varnish used on many original Arts and Crafts pieces.

1. Since the legs and panels have already been cleaned up, you shouldn't have much sanding to do. If necessary, use a random-orbit sander to sand the surfaces to 220 grit. (If you're hand sanding, be careful not to introduce cross-grain scratches where the stiles meet the rails.)

2. After sanding, apply a coat of the pigmented oil finish with a rag (see photo A). Depending on the wood, you may need to apply a second coat on some spots to even out the color.

3. Allow two or three days for the oil finish to cure, then apply two coats of polyurethane. If you don't mind the fumes, the fastest way do this is with a spray can. Brushing would

Craftsman makeover. Dark walnut stain approximates Stickley's trademark finish. More important, it helps the red oak plywood blend with the white oak.

Quick spray finish. Perhaps it's not as thick as a brush-on finish, but spray polyurethane offers protection and extra color.

leave a thicker film, but it may also leave drips in the corners of the piece. As you spray, keep the can parallel to the workpiece and a steady 6" to 12" away from the surface (see photo B). Overlap each painted swath about 50% with the next until the entire surface is covered.

4. After allowing a day for the polyurethane to dry, you're ready to reattach the lid to the bench. If you like the sheen and feel of a wax top coat, you can apply a light coat of wax. Immediately after that, you can throw a few cushions on top and have a seat.

> **WORK SMART**
>
> If the lid of your bench keeps getting bumped against the wall or is dropped in the open position, it can damage the wood, the hinge, or both. To prevent this, consider attaching a small leather strap from one of the side rails to the top of the lid. Make the strap long enough so that the lid can open just past 90°.

Serving Table

This table was designed for kitchens big and small. With a sturdy base and 35 ¼"-high top—a comfortable height for use as a worksurface—it is perfectly suited for chopping, mixing, or other food-preparation chores. It's also attractive enough to use as an extra serving table for drinks or hors d'oeuvres when entertaining a large crowd. On the other extreme, a couple struggling with a cramped kitchen could buy a pair of standard bar stools and use this dining table for everyday meals. With a compact 23 ¾" by 36" footprint, it would also be a nice addition in a sunroom or other small nook.

If this table looks Shaker-esque, it's because it was inspired by the drawings of several different Shaker tables in John Kassay's *The Book of Shaker Furniture* (University of Massachusetts Press, 1980). The clean lines and functionality of the piece are certainly in keeping with the basic Shaker tradition, but the project's beveled top gives it a slightly modern flair. No doubt, true Shakers would be aghast at the sight of a bottom tray designed as a catch-all for miscellaneous kitchen debris. So much for their notion of "a place for everything, everything in its place."

The mortise-and-tenon joinery for the base and the dovetailed tray below offer the perfect opportunity to practice your hand-tool skills and enjoy a few quiet evenings in the workshop. Most of the joinery can be accomplished with a few basic machines, but, honing your favorite plane and a few chisels will make it easier to sneak up on perfectly fitting joints.

What You'll Learn

- Cutting mortises
- Cutting tenons on the tablesaw
- Routing curves with a template
- Cutting tapers on the tablesaw
- Cutting dovetail joinery
- Rubbing out a finish

The joinery for this table looks more difficult than it really is. For example, the base assembly employs mortise-and-tenon joints to lock everything together. You'll learn how to chop a mortise using a drill press and chisel, but if you don't feel up to that task just yet, you'll also learn how to use your tablesaw to tackle the job.

The bottom tray makes use of the quintessential joint of fine woodworking: the dovetail. Don't let the name scare you. Cutting the single-tail joint boils down to making a few short, straight cuts—most of them on your tablesaw. Of course, you can simply rabbet the ends of the tray sides and lock the corners together with dowels and glue.

Chop to it. Drilling out most of the mortise and paring up to the line is easy to master, and easier on your chisel than chopping with a mallet.

This is a more involved project that will require a little more shop time, but you'll learn skills and build a few jigs that will make future projects easier and safer. The edge guide will help you accurately trim this tabletop with a circular saw, but it will also allow you to zip through future long cuts. This jig offers a second edge for use with your router and favorite straight bit. The tenoning jig is another useful project. You'll appreciate the way it hops onto your tablesaw's fence and quickly cuts cheeks in just two passes. Last but not least, you'll learn how to make featherboards to help hold boards closer to blades and bits than fingers should ever go.

When it comes time for finishing, you'll learn how to apply varnish and rub out a finish. Unlike wipe-ons, brushed-on varnish creates a thick film finish that provides better protection from water and food stains. Rubbing out (sanding with progressively finer grits) erases the bumps and bubbles that happen every time you pick up a brush, and it leaves a finish that's showroom smooth.

Tablesawn tails. By adjusting the angle of your sawblade and using a tenoning jig, you can use your tablesaw to make the trickiest cuts of the dovetailed tray.

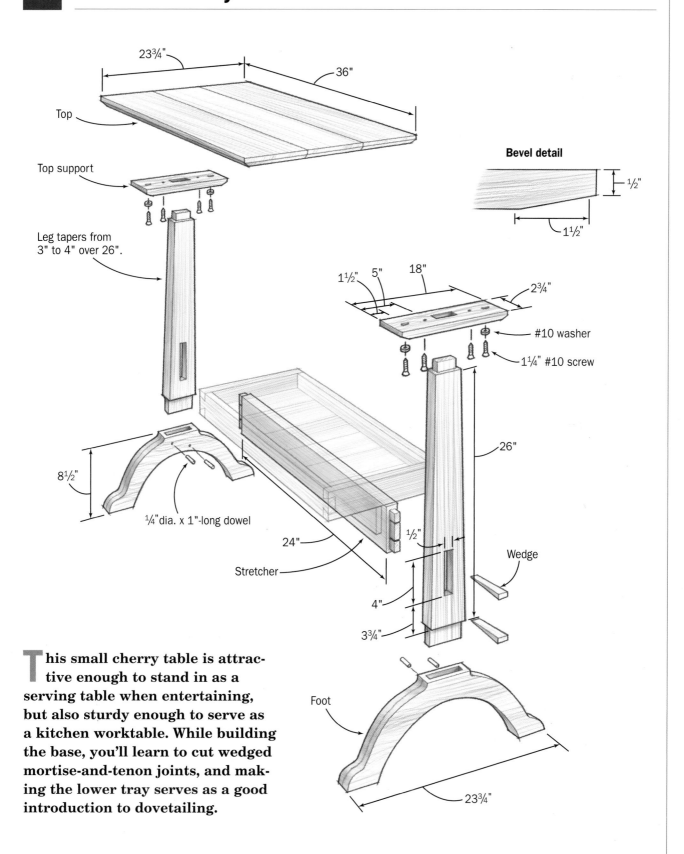

23¾"

36"

Top

Bevel detail

½"

1½"

Top support

Leg tapers from
3" to 4" over 26".

1½" 5" 18" 2¾"

#10 washer

1¼" #10 screw

26"

8½"

¼"dia. x 1"-long dowel

Wedge

24"

½"

Stretcher

4"

3¾"

This small cherry table is attractive enough to stand in as a
serving table when entertaining,
but also sturdy enough to serve as
a kitchen worktable. While building
the base, you'll learn to cut wedged
mortise-and-tenon joints, and making the lower tray serves as a good
introduction to dovetailing.

Foot

23¾"

Quantity	Part	Actual Size	Notes
1	Top	¾" x 23¾" x 36"	All wood is cherry (unless otherwise noted), but a similar hardwood would work as well. You may need three or four boards to make a 23¾"-wide top.
4	Legs	¾" x 4½" x 30"	Face-glue two pieces to make each 1½"-thick leg.
4	Feet	¾" x 8½" x 22"	Laminate two pieces together to make each 1½"-thick foot.
1	Stretcher	¾" x 5" x 27"	
4	Wedges	½" wide x 3" long	Cut wedges from a contrasting wood.
4 pieces	Dowel	¼" dia. x 1"	Can be of the same wood or a contrasting species.
2	Top supports	¾" x 2¾" x 18"	
2	Tray sides	¾" x 3¼" x 20"	
2	Tray ends	¾" x 3¼" x 16"	
1	Tray bottom	¼" x 3¼" x 15½"	Consider using a different wood to contrast sides of tray.
2	Tray supports	¾" x 3½" x 20"	
1 bottle	Polyurethane glue		Foam helps hide small gaps, and dried polyurethane glue is easier to knock off than yellow glue.
1	Natural-bristle brush		Buy a high-quality brush and take the time to clean it well.
2 pieces	Felt		To pad inside face of tray supports.
1 quart	Varnish		See Sources on on p. 170.
1 quart	Varnish thinner		For thinning first coat of varnish and cleaning brush.
	Miscellaneous		120-, 180-, 220-, 320-grit sanding disks (2 of each), 1 sheet 320-grit sandpaper, 1 sheet 600-grit wet-or-dry sandpaper, tack cloth, 0000 steel wool, spray adhesive

Buying Materials

You could build this table from the ¾"-thick hardwood from your home center, but this project offers another good opportunity to visit your local hardwood supplier. Realize that wood at a mill isn't usually ripped in standard widths, but is sold by the board foot. A board foot is the amount of wood contained in an unfinished board 1" thick, 12" long, and 12" wide. This project requires about 20 board feet of material, but you should plan on buying about 50 percent more. That waste factor isn't as wasteful as it may sound. When you finish building this project, you can use the extra material for smaller projects.

You'll need to glue up a few narrower boards to make the top, so board width isn't a concern, but you'll want to pick up at least one 9"-wide by 8'-long board (that's about 6 board feet) to build the feet.

- Tape measure
- Tablesaw with a good rip blade
- Circular saw with a 40-tooth crosscut blade
- Dovetail saw
- Marking knife
- Marking gauge
- Chisel
- Miter saw
- Jigsaw or coping saw
- Sanding drum
- Mill file
- Drill press (optional)
- 12" combination square
- Block and #4 or #5 handplane
- Shoulder plane (optional)
- Card scraper
- Planer (optional)
- Router and router table
- Chamfer and flush-trimming router bits
- Clamps
- ⅛" and ⅜" brad-point drills
- ½" and ¾" Forstner bits
- Drill
- Screwdriver
- Random-orbit sander
- Hand-sanding block (wood block will do)
- 2' level

Building the Table

Like the earlier projects, you can manage this big project by separating it into parts—the top, legs, feet, stretchers, and tray—and finishing each step before focusing on the next. However, you need to think about the "big picture" first. After milling all stock to ¾", lay your boards across your bench (or between two sawhorses) and decide which boards will be used for each part. Pick out the best boards for the top and the next best for the legs and feet. You'll cut the top supports, stretcher, and tray from what's left over. Mark the wood with chalk or a carpenter's pencil to help you remember your choices.

Gluing Up the Top

Because the top is the focal piece of this project, this is not the place to be frugal when selecting wood. Cutting off or avoiding knots or sapwood will cost you a few extra dollars, but it's better than having to stare at a blemish with each morning's cup of coffee.

The top is 23¾" wide to accommodate the maximum cutting width of most benchtop saws. If your saw has a wider cutting capacity, consider bumping up the width to 24".

1. Working from your best boards, choose enough stock to make the top a little wider than the finished dimension—aim for about 27"—and cut three or four pieces to 38" long. The extra length will allow you to stagger the boards a little when arranging them for glue-up.

2. Joint one edge of each board with a handplane or on the tablesaw (see "Skill Builder: Jointing Edges on a Tablesaw on p. 21), then rip and joint the opposite edge. (You still want to make a panel that's 1" or so wider than your finished top.) Dry-clamp the boards before gluing to ensure that there are no gaps along the joints. If everything looks good, you're ready to glue and clamp (see photo A).

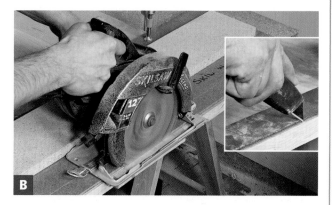

A

Hammered into alignment. You can expect boards in a glued-up panel to shift somewhat as they're clamped tight. With a hammer and scrap block, a few taps can pull the edges flush (before the glue sets).

B

Scored then sawn. When a cut has to count, score the good face with a knife to prevent the blade from splintering the surface. Clamp both ends of the edge-cutting guide to ensure that neither it nor your work shifts in midcut.

3. Once the glue is dry, trim the top to its final dimensions. First, rip one side on your tablesaw to get a clean edge. (If you're using a benchtop saw, this should be about 24".) Next, reset the fence to 23¾" and rip the opposite edge to final width.

4. The top is too wide to crosscut on a tablesaw. Instead, use your circular saw and a straightedge guide. (To learn how to make this jig, refer to "Skill Builder: Making an Edge-Cutting Guide" on the facing page.) To reduce the risk of splintering along the edge, score the cut line with a utility knife (see photo B on p. 77) before cutting. And consider investing in a fresh blade for your circular saw. A 40-tooth thin-kerf crosscut blade is good for most woodworking tasks.

5. Now that the top is trimmed to size, the next step is beveling the bottom edge. This cut is similar to the raised panel used in the blanket box, except that this board is quite a bit larger. If you haven't already done so,

you'll need to increase the height of your rip fence as shown in "Skill Builder: Making an Auxiliary Fence" on p. 41. You may also want to make a few featherboards to help press the stock against the fence while it's fed past the blade. To learn how to make your own featherboards, see "Skill Builder: Making and Using Featherboards" on pp. 80–81.

Tilt your sawblade to 15°, then set your fence so that it's ⅝" away from the bottom edge of the blade (just shy of your finished profile). Use a scrap board to test the cut before cutting the top. Bevel the ends first, then the sides (see photo C).

6. Use a handplane to remove any burns or marks left by the blade. Alternately, you can use sandpaper; just be careful not to round over the edge.

Balancing act. Using a tall auxiliary fence and a featherboard, this cut is safe and easier than it looks. Position a roller stand or sawhorse to support the top at the end of the cut.

Bye-bye to burn marks. Blade marks are unavoidable and easy to deal with. Set your favorite plane to make a light cut and balance the sole on the bevel.

What You'll Need

- ¼" by 12" by 36" hardboard
- ¾" by 5" by 36" plywood or particleboard
- ¾" by 2¾" by 14" plywood
- ¾" screws
- Countersink drill bit
- Drill

This edge guide does double duty. It's designed so that you can run your circular saw against one edge to make perpendicular cuts and your router along the other, for making grooves and dadoes. The T-cleat attached to the bottom of the fence saves time when making perpendicular cuts. Just position the cleat against your stock, align the edge of the guide with the line you're cutting, clamp down both ends, and you're ready to go.

These dimensions aren't critical; you can build this jig from whatever plywood scraps you have on hand. Just make sure your fence has two straight edges and that it is long enough to trim the edge of the table.

Write down what tool and blade or bit you used when cutting the edge of the guide. Using a different router, or simply switching saw blades, can result in a cut that's significantly different than the one you lined up with your guide.

Sliced to the line. The T-square guide ensures that the jig is square to the edge of the table while the hardboard base shows the exact location of the cut.

Doubles as a dado guide. By extending the hardboard base on both sides, you can use the other edge with your router. Remember to use the same router and bit every time you use this guide.

Straight and Square Edge Guide

This simple dado and crosscut jig is built around your router and circular saw. The T-square end positions the guide perpendicular to the edge of your stock, and the hardboard base shows the exact location of the cut.

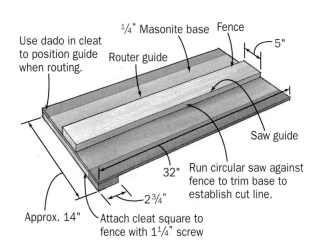

Use dado in cleat to position guide when routing.

¼" Masonite base Fence

Router guide

5"

Saw guide

Run circular saw against fence to trim base to establish cut line.

32"

2¾"

Approx. 14"

Attach cleat square to fence with 1¼" screw

What You'll Need

- ■ ¾" by 4" by 16" piece of plywood or MDF
- ■ Small piece of hardwood
- ■ Glue
- ■ Straight-grained boards, at least 2" wide by 6" long (longer is better)

Featherboards, or fingerboards, are simple jigs that excel at holding narrow or thin stock securely against a table or fence without putting your own fingers at risk. They also prevent kickback and help produce smooth, consistent cuts. Almost any setup where a board is guided past a fence can be both safer and more accurate with a well-placed featherboard.

You can make featherboards in a variety of shapes and sizes.

Featherboard-Making Jig

Clamp this two-board jig to your miter gauge and make your shop a little safer. To adjust the resistance, change the height or spacing of the "feathers."

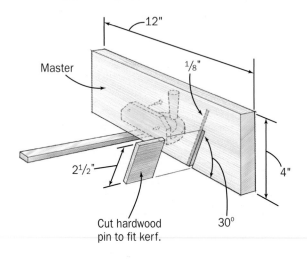

Master

12"

⅛"

4"

2½"

30°

Cut hardwood pin to fit kerf.

1. Set your sawblade to 60°. Because the bevel gauges on the front of most saws can be difficult to read or unreliable, consider using a small drafting triangle to set the blade (see photo A).

2. Clamp or screw your feather "master" to your miter fence. Raise the blade to 2½" and make the first cut. Rip a scrap of hardwood to the exact width of the cut you just made, and glue it into the kerf. (The pin doesn't need to be exactly the height of the cut. It simply provides a registration point as you cut the individual fingers.)

A

Setting the blade. Set the triangle between the carbide teeth and adjust the bevel angle until the blade rests against the plastic triangle.

B

Stronger or springier fingers. The distance from the pin to the cut will determine the spacing between fingers and the amount of give in your featherboard. Start with ⅛" spacing, then adjust to suit your preference.

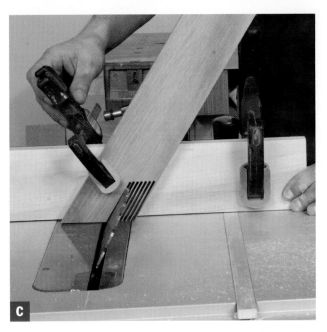

C

Clamps control the cut. Be sure that the clamp is safely out of the blade's path as you make the cuts.

3. Reposition the master so that the pin is roughly ⅛" away from the outside face of the blade and make a second cut as shown in photo B. Realize that the thickness of the fingers affects the flexibility. For a stiffer featherboard, increase the distance between the pin and first cut, or lower the height of the blade.

4. Crosscut the end of your future featherboard to 30°. Next, clamp it against the pin and feed it past the blade. Turn off the saw and wait for the blade to stop. Reposition the board so that the first kerf rides on the pin. Keep cutting fingers (see photo C) for as long as you like. Trim wide featherboards if you need something smaller in the future.

Miter-Slot Featherboards

This featherboard is similar to the one you made earlier, but it is designed to attach to a hardwood bar so that it can lock itself into the miter slot on your tablesaw or router table. To avoid splitting the bar or featherboard when it's tightened in the slot, make both pieces from any straight-grained hardwood.

Drill and counterbore the hole for the machine screw in the bottom bar then use your tablesaw to cut the groove for the featherboard. First, draw a stop line on your board, set your rip fence, and cut along the line. Turn off your saw when the blade is about ¼" from your mark (the blade is cutting farther along the bottom edge). Adjust your fence and make the second cut. Use a coping saw to finish the groove.

Slot-Locking Featherboard

The expanding bar provides adequate clamping pressure to hold the jig on tablesaws, router tables, or any other shop-built jigs with a ¾"-wide slot.

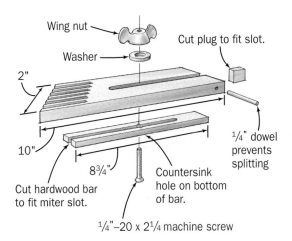

Wing nut

Washer

2"

Cut plug to fit slot.

10"

8¾"

Cut hardwood bar to fit miter slot.

¼"–20 x 2¼ machine screw

Countersink hole on bottom of bar.

¼" dowel prevents splitting

Building the Legs

Gluing up thin boards is a perfectly acceptable way to make the thick stock needed for the legs and feet, but you want to orient the grain so that future wood movement doesn't force open the joint and create an unsightly gap. Wood tends to cup toward the bark side of the tree (if you need proof, take a look any old deck). Arrange the lamination bark side to bark side so that the "inside" face of the tree faces out. (Check the end grain to determine which is the bark side.) That way, if the wood cups, the joint line along the outside edges will stay tight.

1. The 1½"-thick legs are made by laminating two pieces of ¾" stock face to face. Start by cutting four pieces of stock to 5½" x 32". To keep the boards from shifting as you clamp them together, tack two or three brad nails in the center of the lamination, then nip off the ends so just a small point protrudes from the wood. This small point will lock the mating piece into position and keep it from shifting as you tighten the clamps. *Note:* If you plan to rip the lamination to nibble out the mortise (see step 3), position the brads so they won't get hit by the sawblade.

WORK SMART

You can sometimes use screws to apply extra clamping pressure or hold a board in place so you can move a clamp elsewhere. Drill pilot holes so that the screw's threads don't catch the top board; otherwise, the screw won't pull the boards together.

2. Scrape off any dried glue squeeze-out along the edges of the stock, then make a light ripping cut at the tablesaw to establish a straight edge on one side.

3. There are two ways to make the mortise for the stretcher. If you would prefer to go the traditional route, rip the leg to 4½" wide and turn to "Skill Builder: Cutting Through Mortises" on pp. 84–85. Another option is to slice the leg along one side of the mortise, nibble it out with your tablesaw, then glue the pieces back together. The second method is easier, but sharp-eyed critics may see a glue line along the face of the leg.

A

Slip stoppers. Small brads prevent leg pieces from slipping. Drive the nail about ⅛" into the wood, then snip off the head to leave a sharp, short tip.

B

Mortising made easy. By ripping the leg into two pieces, you can treat the mortise like a dado. Clamp the board to your miter gauge and carefully saw up to your layout lines.

Smooth sliced tenons. For wide tenons, a tenoning jig outperforms nibbling away with a dado cutter. The jig cleanly cuts the cheek in one pass, and you won't need to waste time switching blades.

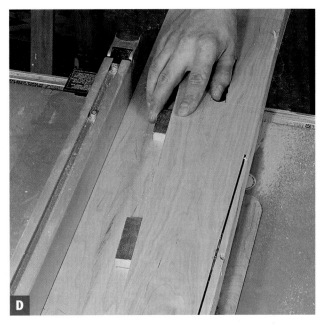

Cutting tapers on a plywood sled. There are slicker tablesaw tapering jigs, but plywood works well enough for a few cuts.

4. To use the rip-and-nibble method, start by jointing one edge. Then, set your saw's fence to 2" and rip off one strip. On the wider piece, lay out the ½"-deep by 4"-long mortise (except now it's a dado) on one face of the leg. Raise your blade to ½" and carefully remove the wood between your lines as shown in photo B on p. 82. When done, reattach the cut strip. Once the glue cures, rip the leg to 4½". When you cut the leg to width, remember to center the mortise on the leg.

5. Once you've completed the mortises, cut the legs to 30". Remember that the bottom of the mortise needs to be positioned so that it begins 6½" up from the bottom end of the leg.

6. The next step is to lay out the taper and the tenons on each leg as shown in photo C. Cut the tenons using your crosscut saw and tenoning jig. For more on this process, see "Skill Builder: Cutting Tenons on the Tablesaw" on pp. 86–87.

7. To taper the leg, use the simplest tapering jig of all—a ¼"-thick by 36"-long plywood sled. First, rip the plywood to 6". Without adjusting the fence, attach the leg to the sled with double-sided carpet tape so that the cut line hangs over the edge of the plywood. (You can attach a few glue blocks with hot glue to secure the leg stock in place.) Adjust the blade height to cut all the way through the leg, then push the assembly past the blade. Use mineral spirits to release the tape and glue bonds. Repeat on the opposite side. Use a handplane or jointer to remove any saw marks.

WORK SMART

When exposed to air and light, cherry's color deepens from a pinkish-tan to a deep red-brown. This change lends a desirable effect unless you have boards that are a few shades different because one was stacked on top of the other. A few weeks in bright sunlight should even out the color.

What You'll Need

- ■ **Combination square**
- ■ **Marking knife**
- ■ **Drill press and Forstner bits**
- ■ **Freshly sharpened chisels**
- ■ **Small piece of hardwood**
- ■ **Two 6" clamps**

Traditionally, mortises are chopped out with just a chisel and mallet. While it's not particularly difficult, it can be slow going, especially if you're trying to make your way through hard or thick stock. Here, you'll learn how to use a drill press to tackle most of the work. After drilling out most of the waste, you can use a chisel to pare to the line. To cut down on some of the chiseling work—which gets old if you're cutting multiple mortises—you can use a router jig for hogging out waste.

1. Establish a centerline, then lay out the location of the mortise. Using a combination square, extend your lines from one face around the edge and onto the opposite face of the board. Use a knife, rather than a pencil, when marking the edges of the mortise. The knife scores the surface of the wood, preventing tearout when drilling, and provides a stop line that you can register against when chiseling.

2. Set up your drill press with the appropriately sized bit. (For narrow mortises, you might use a brad point, but for the ½"-diameter and ¾"-diameter mortises in this project, you'll use Forstner bits.) If your drill press doesn't have a fence, clamp a board to the table so that the tip of the bit runs along the centerline of the mortise. Drill out the ends first and work toward the center, as shown in photo A. It's OK to overlap the drill holes, but position the bit so that the center spur sits in solid wood.

Drilling does the hard work. A small benchtop drill press is fine for taking big bites out of mortises. Clamp a temporary fence in place so that you can concentrate on adjusting the board from side to side.

Calling good backup. Clamping a board against the outside edge of your mortise helps guide the chisel as you make the cut and prevents you from making the mortise too wide.

3. Clamp a hardwood guide along the edge of the mortise and guide the back of the chisel against it to remove the crescents left by the bit (see photo B). To avoid tearing out the opposite face or edge, or overchiseling your mortise, stop when you're halfway through the thickness of the material. Then flip the stock and finish paring out the waste from the opposite side.

OR CLEAN UP WITH A ROUTER

With the jig shown in photo C, you can use your router and a pattern-cutting bit to do most of your cleanup work. The jig takes a few minutes to make, but it can save time if you're cleaning up multiple mortises. Rip a strip of wood to the thickness of the mortise and glue it between two pieces of wood. After drilling out most of the waste, clamp the template in place and feed the router in a counterclockwise direction. You'll still need a chisel to clean up the corners.

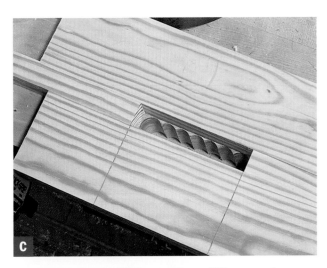

A solution for multiple mortises. When you have more than a few mortises, consider using your router and this simple jig. The bit's bearing rides against the wood while the carbide cutters clean out the mortise underneath.

Building the Feet

Even if you could find 1½"-thick stock, it would still be easier to make the curved feet from a two-piece lamination. For starters, it would be difficult to chop a deep mortise in the top of the foot. Second, a solid foot would be apt to split along a weak grain line. A two-ply leg is less likely to crack.

You'll want to start with a full-size template. Using your template as a tracking guide will ensure that all four boards used to make up the feet are identical. Instead of sanding to the line, use your template to guide a router bit to remove saw marks and finish off the curves.

1. Cut four pieces of ¾" stock to 23¾". (That way, you can get all four pieces from one 8'-long board.) Joint one edge and rip each piece to 8½" wide. Next, use your tablesaw to cut a ⅜"-deep by 3½"-long dado along the center of each board.

2. Cut a spacer just a hair under ¾" thick and 3½" wide to help align the dadoes as you glue up the legs. Wrap the spacer with packing tape so that it doesn't become a permanent fixture as shown in photo B on p. 89.

WORK SMART

Using a template to transfer dimensions to both legs, instead of measuring both legs separately, can prevent measurement errors. Lay out the legs' dimensions, the taper, and the locations of the mortises and tenons on a piece of ¼"-thick hardboard or plywood and cut to the lines.

What You'll Need

- **Crosscut sled**
- **Stop block**
- **Tenoning jig**
- **Tablesaw**
- **Small clamp**

There are several ways to cut tenons, but this one is quick and easy to master. The five-piece tenoning jig shown in the drawing on the facing page can be built in a few minutes, but it works as well as store-bought fixtures costing a lot more.

Using this jig, and your miter fence or crosscut sled, cutting tenons is a two-step operation. First, you'll establish the top, or shoulders, of the tenon. Next, you'll readjust the fence, raise the blade, and cut the sides (also called "cheeks"). You'll learn how to sneak up on a perfect fit using a plane or chisel.

1. Lay out the tenon on your stock and position it on your crosscut sled so that the blade is correctly aligned. Clamp a stop block to the front fence to ensure that the shoulders on the second side (and on all subsequent tenons) are cut to the same height as the first (see photo A). Next, set the height of the blade. To avoid dangling offcuts when cutting the cheeks in the next step, set the blade a hair higher than your layout lines. The overcut will be hidden and won't have a serious effect on the strength of the joint.

Cutting the shoulders. A crosscut sled is good for much more than its name suggests. Adding a stop enables you to use it for cutting tenon shoulders.

Cutting the cheeks. The tenoning jig rides on your saw's rip fence so that the board is completely supported through the cut. For big boards, two clamps are better than one.

2. Place the tenoning jig over the rip fence and adjust the fence to cut along the outside of the line you made for the cheek cut. Adjust the blade height about $\frac{1}{32}$" below the shoulder line. Clamp the stock to the jig, then push the work past the blade as shown in photo B. Turn off your saw before attempting to lift or back up your work. Reposition the board and cut the opposite cheek.

3. A shoulder plane is the best tool for trimming tenons (see photo C), but you can also use a wide chisel. Hold the chisel bevel up, as you would hold a knife. With your other hand, anchor your knuckle against the front edge of the workpiece and pinch the blade with your index finger and thumb. Using your index finger to support the blade and your thumb to control the depth of cut, shave off a thin layer of wood (see photo C inset), then test the fit against the mortise.

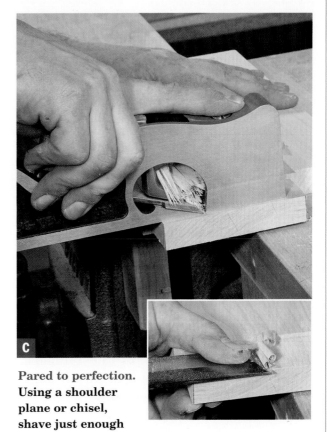

C

Pared to perfection. Using a shoulder plane or chisel, shave just enough wood from the tenon's cheeks so that it slides into the mating mortise with a light tap.

Tenon-Cutting Jig

This jig quickly and smoothly slices tenon cheeks in one pass. The fence prevents tearout on the back face of your work.

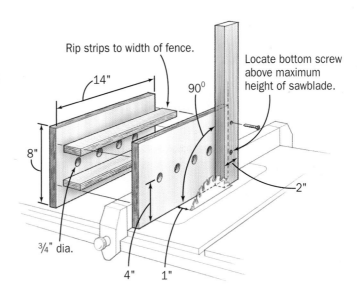

Rip strips to width of fence.

14"

90°

Locate bottom screw above maximum height of sawblade.

8"

2"

$\frac{3}{4}$" dia.

4"   1"

Mortising the feet. After carefully cutting both sides of the dado (later to become a mortise), remove the wood between the cuts by making a few extra passes.

3. While you're waiting for the leg laminations to dry, use the dimensions given in the drawing to draw a full-size copy of half a foot on a piece of hardwood or MDF. Sand and/or file up to your pencil lines. This piece will serve as your template for shaping the feet. (The exact dimensions aren't critical. Just try to make the curves as smooth as possible.)

4. Measure and mark the center of the mortise on the leg blanks, then position and trace the template. To help your bandsaw or jigsaw round the inside corners, drill relief holes in the tightest parts of the curves near the top and bottom of the foot. Try to cut about 1/16" to 1/8" along the outside of the line.

Foot Pattern

Use the given dimensions to establish the top and bottom edges. To establish a pleasing curve, connect those points with a flexible strip of wood.

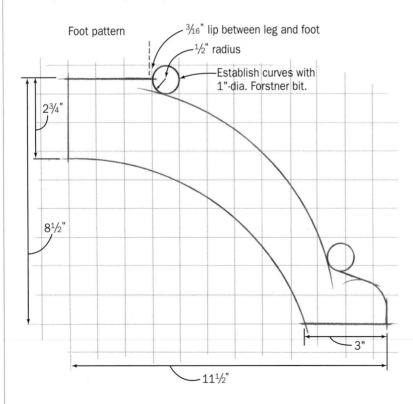

Foot pattern

3/16" lip between leg and foot

1/2" radius

Establish curves with 1"-dia. Forstner bit.

2 3/4"

8 1/2"

3"

11 1/2"

Foot Detail

The dadoes start as a guide when laminating the two pieces of the foot and later become a through mortise once the glue dries.

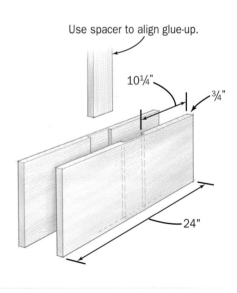

Use spacer to align glue-up.

10 1/4"

3/4"

24"

Screws make good clamp companions. Screws lack the clamping power of bar clamps, but they can hold two pieces tightly together so that you can move clamps where they're needed.

Double-duty template. Made from ¼"-thick hardboard, the template used to trace the legs can also serve to guide a bearing-topped 1½"-long flush trimming bit. When routing, make only light cuts.

5. You can sand or file the saw marks off the foot boards, but if you have a bearing-driven straight bit with the bearing on the far end of the bit, often called a flush-trimming bit, you can use your leg template to finish shaping

the foot at the router table. Attach the template to the foot with carpet tape and adjust the height of the bit so that the bearing rests against the template. Flip the template to shape the other side of the foot.

Building the Stretcher and Top Supports

Use the dimensions given in the materials list and overall drawing as a starting point; but make a habit of transferring dimensions from pieces you've already cut onto the pieces you haven't. You may also want to make the tenons a hair longer than needed, then plane them flush after assembly.

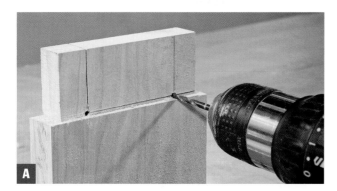

Split stoppers. Drilling a ⅛"-diameter relief hole at the base of the tenon allows the wedge to flare the tenon open (creating a tighter joint) as it's driven in—instead of splitting the stretcher.

The stretcher's tenons should be slightly narrower than the mortises they'll fit into so that the wedges have room to work.

1. To make the stretcher, rip a ¾" board to 5" and crosscut it to 27" long. Lay out and cut the ½"-wide by 4"-long tenons as you did with the legs.

2. Draw the location of the kerfs for the wedges ½" from each end. Drill a ⅛"-diameter hole to serve as a relief hole to prevent the wood from splitting as shown in photo A, then cut the lines with a dovetail saw.

3. To make the wedges, start with a 6"-wide board and cut off a 3"-long piece. Reset your miter saw to make a 5° cut and position the board you just cut so that the end grain (the wide edge) rests against the fence. Cut

Walnut wedges. By setting your miter angle 5° to the right and flipping the piece before each cut, you'll make perfect 10° tapered wedges. The wedge should have a fairly sharp point to fit into the kerf.

the angle on the edge of the board, then flip the board to make a wedge with a 10° angle. Make sure you clamp the stock in place (see

photo B), because doing otherwise would mean holding your hands too close to the blade.

4. Cut two top support pieces to 2¾" by 18". Next, lay out a ¾"-wide by 3"-long mortise on the center of each board. (You can use the rip-and-nibble method as you did with the legs; however, since these mortises will be hidden by the tabletop, chopping these mortises by hand might be a good opportunity to work on your chiseling skills.) After cutting the mortises, use your router table to chamfer the bottom edges, then miter the ends at 45°.

5. The end holes of the supports are designed to allow the top to expand or contract in response to changes in humidity. Position the top supports bottom-face up, and drill four ⅛"-diameter pilot holes. Next, flip the piece and enlarge the end holes by drilling a ¼"-deep by 5/16"-diameter hole. The "flared" bottom gives the screw room to move.

Assembling the Base

You're now ready to assemble the base. Take a moment to hone your favorite chisel—you'll probably have to take few shavings off a tenon or two. Remember to dry-fit each subassembly. Finish-sand (up to 220 grit) any spots that might be difficult to reach once everything is assembled.

1. Apply a light coat of glue to the leg's bottom tenon and slide it into the mortise on the foot. Clamp the assembly so that there's no gap where the two pieces meet. From the inside face, drill two 1"-deep holes with a ¼" brad-point bit as shown in photo A at right. Apply glue to short lengths of ¼" dowels and tap them into place. With that, your

Pegged into submission. Tenons were pegged into mortises long before glue came in neat plastic jugs. Simply drill a hole and tap in a length of dowel that has the same diameter. You can remove the clamps as soon as the dowels are tapped in place.

B

Wedged tight. Driving the wedges flares the end of the tenon, preventing the stretcher from coming loose. When the glue has dried, trim the tenon and wedges, then plane or sand flush with the leg.

mortise-and-tenon joint has turned into what is called a pegged mortise-and-tenon joint. The pegs will keep the joint even more secure. Using a flush-cut saw, trim the dowels flush after the glue has dried.

2. At this point, a dry-fitting should show you legs that are perpendicular to the stretcher and parallel to each other. If not, adjust the tenon shoulders before glue-up. Once you're happy with the fit, glue the stretcher into the legs. Use clamps to squeeze the legs together so that the stretcher's shoulders fit tight against the inside of the legs. Once clamped, wipe a small amount of glue onto the wedges and tap them in place (see photo B). Trim the ends of the tenons and wedges flush.

3. Place the leg assembly on a flat surface—like your workbench—and place the top supports in place. Use a 2' level to make sure the supports are level before gluing them in place.

Building the Bottom Tray

The bottom tray is what makes this project different from any run-of-the-mill table. Besides offering an extra storage shelf, this subassembly gives you the opportunity to show off your woodworking skills. The single dovetailed corner is sure to attract a great deal of attention. And, as you'll see, cutting a dovetail isn't nearly as tricky as it might appear.

You'll need to make a few cuts by hand, but you'll do most of the work with your table-saw. You can adapt the techniques shown here to cut multiple tails, such as for a drawer or blanket chest. For wider panels, consider building a designated crosscut sled, just for cutting the angled tails.

1. Start by ripping a board to 3½" to make the ends and sides of the tray. Crosscut the sides to 20" and the ends to 16". Cut a ¼"-wide by ½"-deep groove along the lower edge on the inside face of the side pieces, as shown in the drawing on p. 92. Cut the boards for the bottom of the tray to 3¼" wide by 15½" long. (You may also substitute a solid piece of ¼"-thick plywood for the bottom.)

Tray Detail

Single-dovetailed corners spice up an otherwise simple box. This mini-project is a good opportunity to practice this classic woodworking joint.

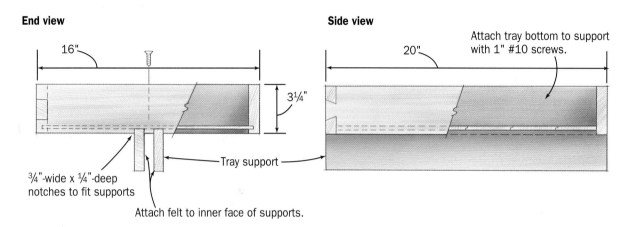

End view

16"

3¼"

¾"-wide x ¼"-deep notches to fit supports

Tray support

Attach felt to inner face of supports.

Side view

20"

Attach tray bottom to support with 1" #10 screws.

2. Using a marking gauge, find the thickness of the sides and ends and add a hair (less than ¹⁄₁₆") to that measurement. Run the gauge around the ends of all four boards. You'll use this baseline to establish the cutting height of the pins and tails.

3. Transfer the dovetail to a piece of cardboard or aluminum flashing to make a longer-lasting guide. On the sides of the tray, line up the shoulder of the template with the baseline you marked with the marking gauge. Then trace tails on both ends (see photo A).

4. Cut the tails on your tablesaw. Clamp the sides to your tenoning jig, then adjust the bevel of the blade until it matches the line. Set the blade height just shy of the shoulder line and make the cut as shown in photo B on p. 93. After cutting both sides, finish the shoulders with a dovetail saw.

5. Clamp the end board in a vise so that the end of the board is slightly above the benchtop, and set the tail board on top. To mark the pins, transfer the location of the tail onto the end grain of the end piece, as shown in photo C. Use a combination square to extend the pencil marks you made on the ends down both faces to the baseline.

A

A tin tail template. Making a template from a scrap of flashing is faster than measuring out the tail on four separate ends. Note how the tail misses the groove for the bottom panel.

Sawn to perfection. Here your tenoning jig does double duty. Adjust the angle of the blade to match the tail, and make the cut. Cut just below the baseline and finish with a handsaw for a tight-fitting joint.

Tracing ensures a tight fit. By using the tails instead of a template, there's no need to worry if your cut is slightly off your original lines. Trace each tail's mating piece.

Three simple saw cuts. Keeping the blade on the waste side of the line, saw as close to the line as you comfortably can. Use a coping saw to remove most of the waste, then pare away the rest with a chisel.

Plane away the evidence. Skewing the plane—so that the blade hits the end grain at an angle rather than straight on—helps slice through difficult end grain.

6. Use a dovetail saw to cut along the waste side of the line, down to the baseline, as shown in photo D. After cutting both sides, remove most of the waste up to the baseline with a coping saw (see photo D, inset) and chisel. Test-fit each corner and shave off any high spots that prevent the tail from fitting between the pins. When test-assembling, pull the pieces straight apart; levering them will affect the appearance of the joint and can snap a pin or tail.

7. Assemble one side of the tray, then slide the bottom panels into the groove. If you made a rabbetted bottom, you may need to trim the panel pieces so they fit between the ends. If that's the case, temporarily remove all the bottom panels, then trim half the excess from the outside edges of the two outermost panels. Doing this keeps the grooves between the boards even.

8. The tails and pins were deliberately cut a little long to make it easier to clean up the joints. The quickest way to do this is with a freshly honed handplane. As you plane across the end grain, work from the edges toward the center (see photo E). If you attempt to plane straight across, you may cause the outside unsupported edge to splinter.

9. Cut the tray supports to size and clamp them to either side of the stretcher. Center the tray on the stretcher and mark the point where the supports intersect the ends. Use a chisel to cut the four ¼"-deep notches so that the tops of the supports are flush with the bottom of the tray. Attach the tray to the supports with glue and eight ¾"-long screws driven through the bottom of the tray.

Custom-fit tray supports. To lay out the notches, clamp the tray supports on either side of the lower stretcher and balance the finished tray on top.

Finishing

Here's how to apply and rub out a varnish top coat to achieve a nice satin sheen. With additional sanding using higher-grit papers and polishing compounds, you can get a high-gloss finish. Just realize that higher sheen will cause even the smallest imperfection to stand out.

Because you intend to abrade the surface, you'll want to use a hard-film-forming varnish.

Technically, polyurethanes and oil/varnish wipe-ons are part of the varnish family, but these finishes are too flexible or don't leave enough of a surface film to be rubbed out. Names that include "rubbing" or "rock hard" are good clues, but to be sure you're using the right stuff: You should find rubbing-out instructions on the back of the can (see Sources on p. 170).

1. Using a random-orbit sander, sand all surfaces up to 220 grit. Use a tack cloth to remove any dust from the project. Wipe down your bench. It's also a good idea to wet-mop your shop floor and put on a fresh work shirt to get rid of dust particles that would otherwise stick to your finish.

2. Mix a batch of varnish 50/50 with thinner to improve the penetration of the first coat. Apply the varnish across the grain, then lightly brush with the grain. After the entire surface has been coated, "tip off" the varnish by lightly dragging the bristle tips through the wet finish. Don't spend too much time trying to level out brush marks; minor ripples should level themselves out or will be sanded down in later coats.

Even scratches make a satin finish. Using 0000 steel wool wrapped around a wood block, rub the perimeter first, then do the center section using long, straight strokes. Try to keep the pressure uniform and your strokes parallel to the grain.

3. Let the first coat dry for at least 24 hours, then sand it using a random-orbit sander outfitted with 320-grit sandpaper. Try not to sand through the first coat; the goal is to knock off bumps and provide some tooth for the next coat. If necessary, use a sanding block to flatten thick drips. Wipe down the surface with a tack cloth before applying the next coat.

4. Brush on a second coat like the first— using long, smooth strokes across the grain to lay on the varnish, then smoothing it out with long strokes along the grain. Continue the varnish/sanding routine for at least three coats. (If you accidentally sand through one of the coats, plan on four or five.)

5. After giving the final coat a week (at least) to cure, knock off any bumps with 600-grit paper. Next, wrap a piece of 0000 steel wool around a sanding block. Rubbing with the grain, make three or four complete passes over the surface, slightly overlapping each pass with the next. Apply a small amount of lemon oil or soapy water to the board to lubricate the steel wool as you give the board a final rubdown. When dry, buff off any remaining haze with a clean rag (see photo on p. 94).

Final Assembly

To protect your top, place a blanket on your bench before laying your top face down. Position the leg assembly so that there's an even overhang along the edges and ends.

Using the previously drilled holes in the top supports as a guide, drill pilot holes in the underside of the top, then screw the base to the top. When driving the screws, back them off about by a ¼ to ½ turn. While you want the top to be securely attached, you should allow for a little wood movement.

Face the inside of the tray supports with felt or thin cork. The lining will make the supports fit a little tighter and will prevent them from scratching the wood.

At this point, you can bring the table in from the shop and make it start working for you. Periodically, wipe on a light coat of wax. Wax provides little protection, but it helps keep stains from sticking. It will also help your project look its very best.

Attaching the top. Use an old blanket to protect the tabletop as you install the final screws. Unless you're careful, dried glue or a few specks of abrasive can wreak havoc on your top in an instant.

Sofa Table

Shopping for furniture can make you feel a bit like Goldilocks. Most pieces are too light, too dark, too tall, or just too expensive; it's rare to find something that's "just right." As a woodworker, you have the unique ability to change the size, color, or material in order to create a piece that's a perfect fit for your home.

This sofa table is an excellent case in point. Built straight from this book, it would look terrific in many homes. Sofa, or console, tables are great for storing books and magazines, showing off collectibles, holding a sound system, or simply offering a reliable spot for keys and gloves. The table's straight lines and solid frame are reminiscent of the Arts and Crafts bench, but the rounded legs and top give it a softer, more contemporary feel, making an easier complement to any room decor. And with a back and interior that's finished as nicely as the sides, you have the freedom to use it anywhere in a room.

But even if you aren't looking for a sofa table, this might be a perfect project for you. This project was designed to lend itself to alteration. By adjusting a few dimensions, you can transform the sofa table into a hall or coffee table. This piece can also be combined with the bookcase in the next chapter to build a hutch, as shown on p. 121. You could also use different woods, plywood panels, or finishes to create a piece that may look entirely different. In truth, though, those differences are only skin deep. After building this table, you may continue to visit furniture stores, but more as a source of inspiration.

What You'll Learn

- **Tablesawn spline joinery**
- **Cutting plywood down to size**
- **Using spacers for perfectly matching double-biscuit joints**
- **Making and installing tabletop fasteners**

By the time you've finished this table—or some variation thereof—you'll have a solid grasp of several important woodworking skills: how to manage big sheets of plywood in a small shop, how to use biscuits and splines for simple, solid joinery, and how to install a solid-wood tabletop that doesn't tear itself apart a few years down the road.

Don't let size fool you. This may be a large project, but it's not difficult to build. When you look at the materials list, you'll discover that each section is made of fewer parts than some of the smaller projects in this book. After assembling each section, simply glue them together to make the case.

Bigger and better than a biscuit. Tablesawn splines fit into the grooves you cut for the plywood panels, locking the assembly together and hiding the groove.

Back-to-back biscuits. Spacers eliminate the need for much math or extra measurements. Here you'll learn how to stack and slot.

While the joinery is similar to what was used to build the Arts and Crafts bench, here you'll use your tablesaw, instead of a router, to cut the grooves for the panels and the ½"-thick by 1"-wide splines used to attach the legs to the rails. You'll still get a chance to use your biscuit jointer, but this time, you'll learn how to cut a super-strong double-biscuit joint. Last but not least, you'll learn how to attach the tabletop to the case using shopmade hardwood buttons. Like store-bought tabletop fasteners, the buttons allow the top to expand and contract in response to seasonal changes in moisture. The difference is that you can make a dozen or more in less time than it takes to drive to the store. Also, you'll have something to show to your woodworking friends who are always crawling under furniture.

Sofa Table with Style and Storage

With a top for displaying photos or a small collection, and a base built to house a small library, this piece could be used against a wall or as a room divider if you don't want to hide it behind a couch.

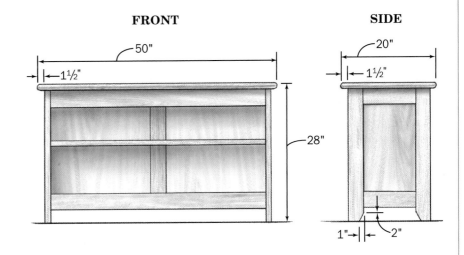

FRONT

50"

1½"

28"

SIDE

20"

1½"

1"   2"

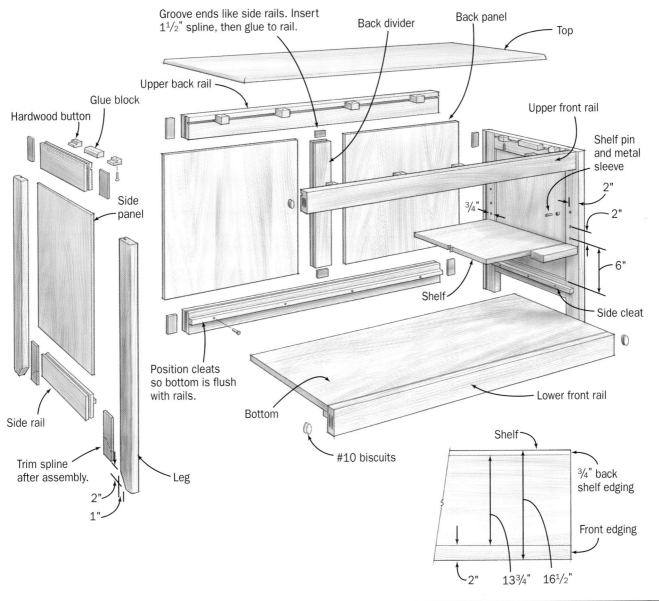

Groove ends like side rails. Insert 1½" spline, then glue to rail.

Back divider

Back panel

Top

Upper back rail

Glue block

Hardwood button

Upper front rail

Shelf pin and metal sleeve

2"

2"

¾"

6"

Side panel

Shelf

Side cleat

Side rail

Position cleats so bottom is flush with rails.

Bottom

Lower front rail

Trim spline after assembly.

Leg

#10 biscuits

2"

1"

Shelf

¾" back shelf edging

Front edging

2"   13¾"   16½"

Quantity	Part	Actual Size	Notes
2	Front and back lower rails	1" x 3" x 45"	
2	Front and back upper rails	1" x 2½" x 45"	Mark the "good" face right away to ensure that the "bad" face is grooved and positioned inside.
4	Legs	1" x 3" x 27¼"	
2	Side rails (lower)	1" x 3" x 12"	
2	Side rails (upper)	1" x 2½" x 13"	
1	Back divider	1" x 2½" x 18¾"	
14	Hardwood splines	1" x ½" x varies	Thickness of strips should be equal to panel thickness. Cut long, then trim after gluing in place.
4	Back panels*	¼" x 22¼" x 19¾"	The eight panels for the sides and back can be cut from one 4' x 8' sheet of ¼" plywood. ½" plywood can also be used.
4	Side panels*	¼" x 13" x 19¾"	
12	Hardwood buttons	¾" x 1" x 1½"	Make a lot now and save them for future projects.
2	Glue blocks	¾" x ¾" x 4"	
2	Front and back cleats	1" x ¾" x 45"	
2	Side cleats	1" x ¾" x 14"	
1	Bottom	¾" x 15½" x 45"	
1	Shelf	¾" x 13¾" x 45"	
1	Shelf back edging strip	1" x ¾" x 45"	
1	Shelf front edging strip	2" x ¾" x 45"	Hardwood hides plywood veneers and prevents shelf from sagging.
1	Top	¾" x 18" x 51"	Earmark your best boards for the most visible part of the table.
4	#10 biscuits		Use with upper front rail.
4	#10 biscuits		Use with lower front rail.
14	Wood screws	1½" #10	For attaching cleats to lower rails
12	Wood screws	1¼" #10	For attaching buttons to top
16	Metal sleeves		For lining shelf pin holes. See Sources on p. 170.
4	Shelf pins		
	Miscellaneous		Yellow glue, polyurethane glue, 150-grit and 220-grit sandpaper, wipe-on polyurethane, polyurethane varnish, 2" foam brush, wax

Buying Materials

For this project, I used 5/4 oak (planed to 1" thick) for the legs and rails and ¾" oak-veneered plywood, reinforced with 1"-thick edging, for the shelves. If you don't have access to a hardwood supplier, you can substitute stair tread stock. You can also make the legs and rails from kiln-dried (2-by) construction lumber jointed and planed to proper dimension. (If you go this route, consider painting the base and splurging for a contrasting hardwood top.)

If you can find sheet goods with two good sides, you may use ½" plywood instead of face-gluing the ¼"-thick panels. Unfortunately, ½" hardwood plywood isn't always available.

- Tape measure
- Tablesaw with a good rip blade and dado cutter
- Miter saw
- Two (preferably four) 50" panel clamps
- Biscuit jointer
- 12" combination square
- Block and #4 or #5 handplane
- Card scraper
- Flush-cut saw
- Router
- Chamfer and ⅜"-diameter roundover bits
- Clamps
- ⅛"-diameter, ⅝"-diameter, and countersink drill bits
- Drill
- Screwdriver

Building the Sofa Table

When building a larger project, it helps to envision it in sections. With this table, I grouped the legs, rails, and stiles (and center divider) in three separate piles. With a quick glance, I could instantly tell which boards had been cut and which hadn't. Take extra time to make sure that your measurements are accurate on the first piece, then rely on your tools' fences and stops rather than marking out every board. This will not only save time but also avoid small errors that can add up to big mistakes.

Cutting the Case Parts

1. To make boards easier to handle, start by cutting them to rough length (roughly an inch longer than the final dimensions in the materials list on p. 100). Cut four boards to 46" to make the front and back rails. Next, cut the leg stock 28" long. You can leave the two side rails together for now—just cut two boards to 26" long. The longer board will be easier to handle on your tablesaw. Crosscut the rails to length after ripping them to width and cutting the grooves.

2. Joint one edge of each board. If you don't own a jointer, refer to "Skill Builder: Jointing Edges on a Tablesaw" on p. 21.

3. Rip the pieces to exact width after jointing. Set your fence and make all the same-size cuts

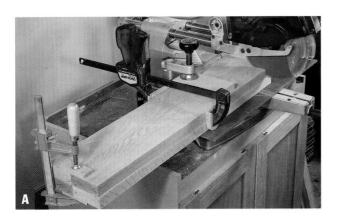

Four legs in one pass. Stack cuts and stop blocks help prevent the dreaded "wobbly table syndrome" and ensure that all your legs turn out exactly the same length.

Miters made simple. This simple jig attaches to your miter saw's fence, enabling you to cut acute angles along the ends of boards. Make sure the clamp is clear of the blade before you make the cut.

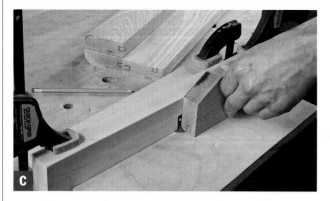

Routing on edge. Using a ⅜"-diameter roundover bit and a router table, rout the outside edges of the legs. Adjust the height of the bit and location of the fence to create the smoothest possible curve.

at the same time. Rip the legs and bottom rails to 3" wide. Reset your fence to 2½" and rip the top rails and center divider.

4. As you crosscut the boards to length, try to take as few measurements as possible. For example, if you're using a sliding compound miter saw (or are using a crosscut sled), clamp several pieces together and cut them in one pass as shown in photo A on p. 101. For miter saws, measure and cut the first piece, then use it as a guide to position a stop block.

5. Using the drawing on p. 99 as a guide, lay out a taper on the bottom of one leg. You could use a tablesaw to cut the leg, but short tapers like this are easier to cut on a miter saw. Refer to photo B on p. 101 and the drawing on the facing page, to build a simple jig to hold the stock perpendicular to the saw's regular fence.

A Handy Marking Method

When making multiple parts, such as these legs, you'll see that some parts are identical, while others are mirror images of each other. Routing and/or grooving the wrong side could leave you with too many "rights" and not enough "lefts." One way to prevent this is by marking the top ends (as shown) to remind you what gets cut where. Penciled-in cut and rout lines on the top ends of the legs provide valuable reference when flipping parts around from machine to machine.

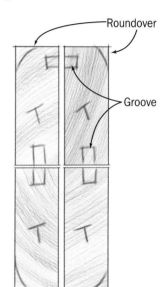

6. Routing the leg stock on edge, as shown in photo C, produces a slightly different profile than making the same cut with the face of the leg against the table. Test the bit on a piece of scrap wood. If one side has a "flat," adjust the fence or base to expose more bit; back off the bit if there's a stepped or beaded edge.

Making the Plywood Panels

As with the Arts and Crafts bench, you'll use ¼"-thick plywood for the back and side panels, but here you will laminate two pieces together to make a ½"-thick panel. This isn't for strength, but aesthetics. Unlike

the bench, there's no way to hide a "bad" side—you want the interior to look as nice as the exterior. Avoid plywood that has cracks or obvious repairs to the surface veneer.

Most miter saws are not designed to cut much past 45°. Trying to push the end of a board against the fence—for example, to nip the bottom ends of these legs—is not only inaccurate, but potentially dangerous. This jig offers a much safer solution. It sets a fence perpendicular to the one already on your saw, allowing you to cut miters from 45° up to 90°. Toggle clamps can be used with other jigs when this one's not in use.

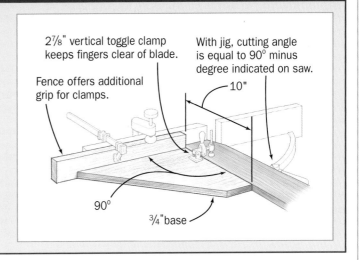

2⅞" vertical toggle clamp keeps fingers clear of blade.

With jig, cutting angle is equal to 90° minus degree indicated on saw.

Fence offers additional grip for clamps.

10"

90°

¾"base

1. To make large panels more manageable, it helps to cut them to rough dimension first. To learn a few different methods for cutting plywood, refer to "Skill Builder: Cutting Plywood" on pp. 104–105. First, rip a 14" by 96" strip for the four side panels, then crosscut it to rough length. Next, measure off the remaining factory edge and rip a 24"-wide strip for the four back panels. Crosscut both strips to make a total of eight panels that are approximately 20" long.

2. At your bench, inspect the rough-cut panels. Arrange the pieces to achieve the most attractive grain match (inside and outside the case). After determining the interior and exterior faces, and what should be glued to what, spread a thin coat of glue onto the "bad" faces and glue the panels together as shown in photo A. It's okay if the panels slide around a little; at this point they're slightly oversize.

3. Once the glue cures, use your tablesaw or circular saw and straightedge (refer to "Skill Builder: Making an Edge-Cutting Guide" on p. 79 to trim the laminated panels to final dimension).

4. Sand both faces of each panel up to 220 grit, being careful not to sand through the thin surface veneer. To help the panels slide into the grooves, plane a light chamfer along the ends and edges of both sides. If you plan to stain your bookcase, stain the panels now; otherwise minor glue squeeze-out may leave unstained spots where the panels meet the legs or rails.

A

Gluing up the panels. **Spread a thin film of glue on each face, then sandwich the two panels together. You don't need a lot of clamping pressure; paint cans will do fine.**

What You'll Need

- **Tape measure**
- **Chalkline**
- **Circular saw**
- **Straightedge guide**

A circular saw can make unwieldy panels manageable. Don't worry if all your cuts aren't exact. Like many situations in woodworking, cutting plywood is all about knowing which cuts count and which ones don't. Here, you'll first use your circular saw to rough-cut the panels, then your tablesaw to trim the panels to size. But rough doesn't necessarily mean inaccurate. To reduce waste, learn to make your cuts as straight as possible. It's also important to be mindful of the factory-cut edge so that it can be used later as a reference when ripping on the tablesaw or when crosscutting with a T-square guide.

RIPPING PLYWOOD

The trick to cutting big panels is to provide plenty of support to both sides of the cut. The easiest way to do this is to buy a 4' x 8' sheet of insulating foam board and make the cut on the ground. The foam is sturdy enough to support you and the plywood, enabling you to get behind your saw comfortably.

1. Use a chalkline to establish your cut line. Measure the cut on both sides of the panel, hook the line on the far end, then pull it across so that the string rests on both marks. Pull the string taut, then give it a light pluck (see photo A).

2. Set the blade depth so that the teeth barely score the foam, and position yourself so that you can see the front end of the blade as you make the cut.

A

Snap to it. An inexpensive chalkline is almost as accurate as a laser, but it doesn't require batteries.

B

Rip to the line. The foam backboard protects the blade from carbide-concrete contact. Set the sawblade so that the teeth just touch the foam.

If you start to drift too far from your line, stop the saw. Trying to steer back to the line could cause the saw to kick back toward you. Instead, reposition the saw over the line, hold open the blade guard, plant the front end of the saw's base on the plywood, then lower the back of the base to plunge into the cut (see photo B).

CROSSCUTTING PLYWOOD

Plywood is made of several layers of wood with the grain running in alternating directions, so in truth you're only crosscutting the top veneer and every other ply. These same techniques also work for making accurate rip cuts with the grain.

1. An edge guide is a fast and accurate way to cut wide panels. Measure the cut on both sides and position the guide to connect the dots. If want your cut to be perfectly perpendicular to the edge, and are using the T-square guide described in chapter 4 "Skill Builder: Making an Edge-Cutting Guide" on p. 79, try to position the guide against a factory-cut edge. A sawn edge may not be straight enough to provide an accurate reference (see photo C).

2. When using a tablesaw, a panel may be too wide for you to use your miter gauge, or too long for you to use your rip fence. Here's another reason to build the crosscut sled shown on pp. 44–45.

For long strips, build a support strip for your saw, like the one shown below. The strip is the same thickness as the crosscut sled. It helps support the offcut so that you won't have to struggle to hold the panel flat against the base of the sled (see photo D).

C

Straight crosscuts. Use a straightedge guide to crosscut wide panels. You may want to make a longer guide to cut panels up to 4'.

D

Sled assistance. A crosscut sled is a reliable way to accurately crosscut wide panels. Add a spacer to support the plywood so that it doesn't bow as you make the cut.

By using different woods and panel products, you can easily adapt this project to fit almost any style of room. Pictured from left to right: "classic"—oak rails with oak panel; "contemporary"—painted poplar with Masonite; "cottage"—poplar with beadboard paneling; and "country"—milk-painted poplar with birch paneling.

Grooving the Legs and Rails

You're now ready to switch out your rip blade and install a dado cutter. You'll barely need to change the dado height or the fence for the next six steps. The legs, rails, and center dividers are grooved with four small changes to the location of the fence, and just one adjustment to the cutter height.

1. Replace your sawblade with a dado cutter and attach a plywood auxiliary fence. Insert only the inner and outer blades. Rather than trying to adjust the width of the cutter and then having to center it on the board, make the groove in two passes.

2. Adjust the cutter so that it is approximately ¼" high. Slide the rip fence so that the cutter is roughly centered on the board. Make your first pass, then flip the board so that the opposite face is against the fence and make a second pass. Compare the width of the groove you just cut with the thickness of two pieces of ¼" plywood. Adjust the fence in small increments until the two pieces of your plywood paneling fit snugly.

WORK SMART

Depending on the hardness of the wood, your saw's motor, and the condition of your dado blade, your saw may not like plowing ½"-deep and ¼"-wide dadoes through hardwood in a single pass. If your saw sounds like it's straining, or if it feels like you need extra oomph to feed the board past the blade, make the cut in two ¼" steps.

3. Raise the cutter to a hair above ½" (to give the plywood a little wiggle room) and groove the inside edges of the legs, the inside edges of the back rails, and both edges of the back divider as shown in photo A on the facing page. Do not groove the front rails.

4. Without adjusting the height of your dado cutter, replace your auxiliary fence with your tenoning jig. (If you made your auxiliary fence and tenoning jig from the same material, you may not need to adjust your rip fence, but check to be sure.) The groove along the end should be even with the edge grooves.

As you did along the edges, groove both ends of the four side rails, two back rails, and back divider in two passes (see photo B).

5. The back rails are inset by ¼" into the back leg. This creates some visual interest, and it's easier to hide a less-than-perfect joint than if the pieces met flush on the outside edge. To cut this groove, don't touch the dado height; simply set your fence so that the groove starts ⅝" from the back edge. Cut the inside faces of both back legs as shown in photo C, then adjust the fence to widen the groove so that you can fit the two-ply plywood panel. (Note that the bottom of the groove will be concealed with a hardwood spline as you assemble the case.)

6. After cutting the grooves for the plywood panels, use your dado cutter to make a shallow groove on the inside face of all four top rails for the wood buttons used to attach the top. Lower the dado cutter to ⅜" high, and adjust the fence so that the groove starts ⅜" in from the top edge. Groove the top edge of all four top rails: the front, back, and side top rails. After the first pass, adjust the fence to widen the groove to ⅜" and make a second pass.

WORK SMART

Plane off any blade marks and sand the legs and rails up to 220 grit before assembly. You'll need to spot-sand a few spots later on, but it's faster and easier to clean up the boards now, rather than after it's assembled.

Grooving the ends. Use your tenoning jig to support the back rails and back divider as you groove the ends for the hardwood splines.

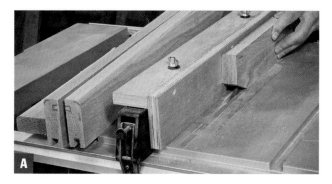

Cutting a centered groove. Flipping the stock and cutting the groove for the panels in two passes ensures that it is centered on your stock.

Back panel groove. Using your dado cutter, mill a groove along the inside face of both back legs to fit the back panel and ½"-thick splines to attach the legs to the back rails.

Making a double-biscuit joint

ingle-biscuit joints are good for alignment, but there's not enough material
in them to provide significant mechanical strength. A double biscuit, however, is
almost as strong as a traditional tenon, and
much easier to cut. By using your benchtop
as a reference surface, and ¼"-thick hardboard spacers to raise the cutter, it's easy
to establish a ¼" offset between the leg and
front rails and accurately position two
biscuits in each joint. If at first the spacer
trick seems confusing, practice on a piece of
scrap wood.

Note that you will use #10 biscuits for
the bottom rail and smaller #0s for the top.
There's no harm done if you accidentally
forget to switch from #0 to #10; it's just a
smaller slot. But if you have the jointer set to
#10 as you cut the top rail, the blade will cut
through the edges of the board.

1. Start with the legs. Butt the two front legs
together so that the inside face is up. Use

WORK SMART

iscuits are made from compressed wood
and are designed to expand when they come
in contact with glue. If you live in a humid
area and have repeatedly forgotten to close
the lid of their container, biscuits may expand
prematurely and become too thick to fit in
the slots. If this happens, you may need to pick
up a fresh can.

your combination square to mark the locations of the upper and lower rails. Find the
midpoint and draw a reference line for your
biscuit jointer. Next, position the leg on your
bench, front edge down. Place two ¼" spacers
under the base of the mortise, align the cut-
line on the jointer with the reference line you
made on the leg, and cut the first slot. Add a
third spacer and cut the second slot as shown
in photo D. Repeat with the other leg.

D

Biscuiting the leg. When cutting the first slot,
use two biscuits to raise the biscuit jointer of the
bench. Adding the third establishes a ¼" space
between the two slots.

E

Cut the slots. The front edge of the leg is offset
from the rail by ¼", but the biscuits are sure to
line up if you use ¼"-thick spacers when you cut
the biscuits. Using one spacer, cut the first slot,
then add the second spacer to cut the other slot.

2. To cut the slots in the rails, mark a centerline to position the biscuit jointer. This time, you'll only need two spacers. Position the top rail against your bench, outside face down, and set your biscuit jointer to #0.

Place one spacer under the jointer and make the first cut. Next, add a second spacer and make the second cut as shown in photo E. Adjust the depth adjustment to #10 and repeat the process with the bottom rails.

Assembling the Panels

Before assembling the table, you'll need to cut a few splines. The splines lock the case together and conceal the exposed grooves you cut to install the panels.

Glue the splines into the leg/rail grooves using polyurethane glue. Dried polyurethane glue is much kinder to chisels and planes than dried yellow glue. Yellow glue, however, is a better choice for gluing the panels in place and for the biscuited rails. Wipe up excess yellow glue before it cures, but wait until polyurethane dries before cleaning it.

1. Switch back to your rip blade and set the fence to cut a strip as wide as the thickness of two pieces of ¼" plywood. Using leftover stock from the legs or rails, cut about a half dozen 12"-long splines. Leave them long for now. As you assemble the panels, save the cutoffs to use on the next assembly.

A

Cut the splines with a push stick. **This simple jig prevents kickback and keeps fingers out of the way as you feed the stock past the blade.**

Ripping thin strips can be dicey; you don't want your fingers near the blade, nor do you want the strip between the blade and fence to tilt into the saw and shoot toward you. If you don't already have one, build the push stick shown in photo A, and in "Jig: Renewable Push Stick" on p. 110.

B

Gluing the side panel. **Once the panel is clamped in place, apply polyurethane glue to the splines and slide them into the grooves where the legs meet the rails.**

C

Gluing the back panel. **Not all big assemblies are hair-raising. Gluing the back panel together now will make assembling the case much easier. Use spacers to ensure that the rails remain parallel.**

D

Patched to perfection. **The tight-fitting splines attach the rails to the legs and hide the groove you cut for the side panels. Saw off most of the wood, then pare or plane flush.**

2. You are now ready to begin assembly. Start with the smaller side panels first. On your assembly table (see "Skill Builder: Building a Self-Squaring Assembly Table" on p. 63), apply glue to the grooves along the edges of the legs and side rails. Slide a panel in place and clamp the side assembly against the squaring strip. (If your assembly table doesn't have squaring strips like the one shown, use a framing square or drafting triangle to make sure the rails are perpendicular to the legs.)

After clamping the side assembly, apply a light bead of polyurethane glue to the splines and slide them into the grooves along the top and bottom of each leg as shown in photo B on p. 109. Use a small clamp to seat the spline against the bottom of the groove.

3. Before assembling the back assembly, cut two 1½"-long strips to join the end of the back divider to the top and bottom rails. The short splines don't add much strength; their real purpose is to align the divider to the rails.

JIG: RENEWABLE PUSH STICK

In theory, if you keep replacing the base and push bar, this push stick will last forever. This jig is particularly useful for cutting thin strips, like the ½"-thick splines used here. The flat base directs even pressure onto the face of the board, not just the back edge, which could cause the wood to twist into the blade at the end of a cut. The sacrificial push bar also prevents kickback by sliding both sides of the board safely past the blade.

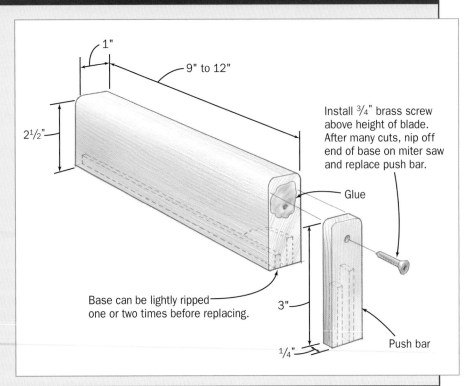

1"

9" to 12"

2½"

Install ¾" brass screw above height of blade. After many cuts, nip off end of base on miter saw and replace push bar.

Glue

Base can be lightly ripped one or two times before replacing.

3"

¼"

Push bar

4. The back is glued together like the two side panels, but you may need to make some changes to deal with the size of the glue-up. In this case, the 46"-long panel was too long for the squaring strips on my assembly table. I extended one strip by adding two strips of wood, as shown in photo C on p. 109. I also cut a groove in a longer piece of scrap to help align the ends of the rails while maintaining a ½" plywood lip.

In addition to a framing square or drafting triangle, you may want to cut two 18¾"

spacer strips, like the ones shown shown in photo C on p. 109. These spacers are the same length as the back divider. Positioning them on the back panel, one at each end, ensures that the top and bottom rails are parallel.

5. As soon as the polyurethane foam isn't sticky, trim the splines. Use a flush-cut or dovetail saw to remove most of the material as shown in photo D on p. 110, then finish up with a plane or chisel.

Pulling the Case Together

1. Now that the panels are assembled, you're ready to turn these pieces into a case. Place one side assembly on a flat surface. Spread a thin bead of glue in the back groove of the leg and insert the back panel. Use a pair of squaring triangles to support this assembly as you glue and attach the opposite side

panel. For more on squaring triangles, see "Jig: Squaring Triangles" on p. 67.

2. Apply polyurethane glue to the splines and insert them into the grooves in the back upper and lower rails. Trim flush when dry.

3. The bottom rests on ¾"-wide cleats that run along the inside edge of the bottom rails. Use a combination square to establish a line ¾" (thickness of the bottom) down from the top edge of the rails. Drill pilot and countersink holes into the cleats as shown in photo F, then attach them with 1¼"-long screws.

E

Taking it down a notch. If you're running out of ceiling space, or can't reach the far end of your clamps, a piece of particleboard or plywood on your shop's floor can double as an assembly table.

F

Attach the cleat. Once positioned, clamp the cleat in place to prevent it from shifting when you tighten the screws.

4. You may need to make a few adjustments to the dimensions in the Materials List in order to make the bottom fit the case. Next, adjust your tablesaw to make a $\frac{1}{16}$"-deep cut and score the top edges of the bottom panel. This line, as shown in photo G, hides minor imperfections and creates a visual break so that you don't draw unwanted attention to the spot where the plywood's grain clashes with the top edge of the bottom rail.

Clean and simple cut line. As seen on the assembled case, cutting a small notch along the top edge of the bottom panel helps hide minor gaps or unevenness.

Making and Installing the Shelf

To keep with the solid look of the rest of the table (and to use some leftover material), edge both sides of the middle shelf with 1"-thick stock, then rout the top edge to match the legs. Besides hiding the plywood edge, the wood strips also strengthen the shelf. For additional edging techniques, refer to "Skill Builder: Building Sag-Free Shelves" on p. 127.

1. Cut the shelf to length (about $\frac{1}{8}$" shorter than the bottom rail so that you can get it in and out of the case). Next, attach 1"-thick edging to both sides. Try to keep the edging flush with the "good" side of the shelf as you tighten the clamps. If necessary, sand or plane the top edge flush when dry.

2. Rip a small groove on the other side of the top face, where the edging meets the plywood, to match the bottom. Rout the top edge of the shelf to match the leg profile.

3. The shelf rests on simple brass pins. To prevent wobble, make sure that the holes are at the same height in all four corners. To do this, use a simple drilling template made from

O marks the spot. Spiral reinforcement patches mark the location of the pin holes, but paint works just as well. Drilling through a wood block serves as a more reliable depth gauge than a piece of tape.

SIZING SHELF-PIN HOLES

The size of shelf-pin holes depends not only on the pins, but also on the material you're drilling into. The same pin may need a slightly larger hole for hardwood than softwood or plywood. To be safe, drill a test hole in a piece of scrap before drilling an entire row in your project.

a scrap of ¼" pegboard as shown in photo B. (See " Jig: Shelf-Drilling Guide"on p. 129).

When using a piece of pegboard to drill the shelf-pin holes, be sure not to drill too close to the edge of the leg. Position the pin holes so that the pins support the plywood, not the wood strips. That way, the pins will hide behind the edging.

4. The metal sleeves prevent the pins from wearing out the holes. They also hide minor tearout caused by the bit. The sleeves are press-fit in place (see photo B). If a pin feels loose, a drop of cyanoacrylate (aka Krazy Glue®), will help lock it in place.

Press-fit sleeves. Metal sleeves prevent the pins from widening the holes and can help hide minor tearout left by the bit. Depending on the hole, some may require a few mallet taps.

Building the Top

The top is a fairly straightforward two- or three-board glue-up. But you'll use your standard ⅜"-diameter roundover bit to make a more distinctive edge profile, and attach the top to the case using wood buttons instead of metal fasteners.

1. Cut the boards for the top a little longer than needed so you can slide them around to get a good grain match. Once you're happy with the arrangement, mark the boards, joint one edge, and glue up. When dry, rip the panel to width and crosscut it to length. Sand the top to 220 grit.

2. If you haven't grown tired of the basic roundover yet, you will. By making a slight change to the height of the bit as you rout the top and bottom edge, you can create a more distinctive bullnose profile. When routing, remember to rout the ends first, then the sides. Any minor tearout along the ends will be cleaned up when you rout the sides.

Making a Bullnose Edge

You can make custom profiles from a regular roundover bit simply by changing the height of the cutter.

Step 1: Adjust height until bit grazes top edge.

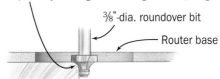
⅜"-dia. roundover bit
Router base

Step 2: Lower bit to maximize roundover, but do not rout bead, or "lip," on bottom edge.

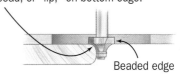
Beaded edge

3. Lay the top on the case so that the edges overhang the front, back, and sides by 1½". Use wood buttons to attach the top to the case (refer to "Skill Builder: Making Tabletop Fasteners" on pp. 114–115). Use a clamp to

What You'll Need

- **6" (or wider) scrap of ¾"-thick wood**
- **Dado blade**
- **Drill with ⅛"-diameter and countersink bits**
- **Wood screws**

There are numerous aftermarket solutions for attaching tabletops, but I think wooden buttons look more refined. Plus, you can make a few dozen from scrap wood in less than an hour. Buttons, or fingers, are simply L-shaped blocks that are screwed to the bottom side of the tabletop. The button fits into a groove or mortise cut in the inside of the rails (or aprons on tables). As the top expands and contracts, the buttons can move in the groove and still hold the top in place. Buttons do not need to be the exact dimensions shown here, but this is a convenient size. Consider making a few dozen now to save time when assembling future projects.

1. Start with a ¾"-thick board that's at least 6" wide. Using your tablesaw or router table, cut a ⅜"-deep by ½"-long rabbet along both ends (see photo A).

2. Using your miter saw, set a stop 1½" from the blade and trim off both rabbetted ends (see photo B). Continue rabbetting and trimming your board until you have all the strips you want, or the board gets too short to cut.

Cut a slice of buttons. Set up a stop block to 1½", then use your saw. If your saw cannot crosscut a wide board, notch a few narrower boards so that you have enough stock for the following steps.

Notching the buttons. Since the notch runs all the way to the end, use your auxiliary fence to keep your fence a safe distance from the dado cutter.

Cutting buttons. The sacrificial fence prevents the small cutoff from getting sucked back by the blade. The blade should stop completely before raising it from the cut.

Homemade Tabletop Fastener

Hardwood buttons are strong enough to hold a top securely in place, but also flexible enough to allow the panel some freedom of movement should the wood expand or contract.

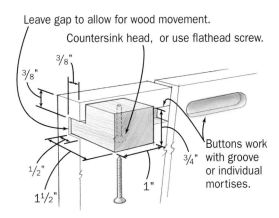

Leave gap to allow for wood movement.
Countersink head, or use flathead screw.

3/8"
3/8"
3/8"
1/2"
3/4"
1"
1 1/2"

Buttons work with groove or individual mortises.

A

Buttoning down the top. Unlike some tabletop fasteners, wood buttons hold the top securely but still allow for wood movement. Space buttons about 6" apart.

hold the top to the rail as you drill pilot holes for the buttons, then screw them in place (see photo A).

3. Drill a pilot hole in the strip. Size the hole so that the threads of the screws spin freely. You'll want the screw to bite into the top, not the button. If you wish, you can also countersink the button.

4. Back at your miter saw, set a stop to nip off a 1"-wide button. If you do not have a zero-clearance fence, there's a good chance that your miter saw's blade will catch and toss this small cutoff. To prevent this, clamp a piece of scrap wood in front of the fence, as shown (see photo C on the facing page). Allow the blade to come to a complete stop before raising it from the cut. When cutting the buttons, try not to slice through the scrap wood. Also, allow the blade to come to a complete stop before raising it from the cut.

Finishing Touches

Oak really doesn't need a lot of help to look good. But before bringing the table into your family room, you should remove the top and apply one or two coats of wipe-on polyurethane to the interior and exterior surfaces. The top should be finished to withstand slightly more use and abuse, such as water from plants, wet gloves, and coffee cups. To provide extra protection, I applied two coats of wipe-on polyurethane, as on the rest of the case, then brushed on an additional coat of regular polyurethane. Whatever finish you choose, be sure to coat the bottom and top surfaces evenly to prevent the panel from cupping later on. Once finished, reattach the top and install glue blocks for a little extra insurance.

Bookcase

With catalogs, office supply houses, and furniture stores offering shelves and bookcases in every imaginable size and style, you might wonder why you'd want to build one from scratch. Store-bought shelving can be attractive, quick and easy to assemble, and surprisingly affordable. The catch is that most aren't really designed to store books; what manufacturers call "oak" or "cherry" is too often a photo-laminate concealing a particleboard core. After a few years—at best—these store-bought shelves start to sag, or the support pins tear out of their holes. Either event can lead to a delightful cascade of books, usually at 2 a.m.

If you have grown tired of flipping bowed shelves like a tired, old mattress, look no further. This bookcase was built to last. As with the sofa table, ½"-thick plywood panels are glued into ½"-deep grooves, reinforcing the rails and stiles just like the center web on a steel I-beam. By buttressing both edges with 1½"-wide wood strips, the plywood shelves are as sturdy as solid hardwood, but easier (and less expensive) to build. Finally, the metal-sleeved shelf pins used to support the shelves eliminate the dreaded "wobbly pin" syndrome.

One big benefit of building this bookcase instead of buying one ready-made is that, like the sofa table, it can be customized to fit any space. Taller bookcases may work well in an office or study, but a pair of shorter cases are a good way to create a small reading nook. You can also think of it as the first piece in a whole-room shelving system. As your library grows, you can add different-sized units without the fear that your favorite style has been discontinued or is "temporarily out of stock."

This same bookcase can also be stacked onto the sofa table from the previous chapter to make a handsome hutch (see the photo on p. 121).

What You'll Learn

- **Edging plywood**
- **Building sag-free shelves**
- **Choosing shelf-hanging hardware**
- **Installing adjustable shelves**

This bookcase is more than just a bookcase. Like the sofa table, this project offers the opportunity to learn techniques that will enable you to design and build case pieces of almost any size. You'll use your tablesaw to cut the grooves for the plywood panels and prepare the rails and stiles for simple but solid spline joints in a way that guarantees that all the cuts line up. Another advantage to using splines is that you can cut your parts to size without factoring in extra wood to create the joint.

You'll also learn to design and install shelving. The difference between a solid shelf and one that sags like an old horse depends on several factors: the size of the shelf, your choice of material and edging, how the shelves are attached to the sides, and what you intend to store. Understanding the basics will prevent problems on future projects and may even help you revive some of the less-than-perfect shelving in your house.

This is a big project, but not terribly complicated if you think of it in parts: sides, back, shelves, and top. You'll assemble the sides and back to make three large frames that are clamped together to build a box. Then, it's simply matter of screwing on the top and installing the shelves. Each of these steps could easily be accomplished in a weekend, with time left over to tackle other chores.

Peg perfection. Drilling shelf holes isn't rocket science, but you'll learn a few simple tricks that will ensure your shelves stay steady.

Better edging with biscuits. You've learned how to use your biscuit jointer to do some fancy joinery. Here, you'll learn how it can be used to make solid wood edging a snap to install.

Built for Books

The ½"-thick plywood panels are glued into grooves cut in the rails and stiles, providing additional strength and rigidity for the 1"-thick hardwood frame.

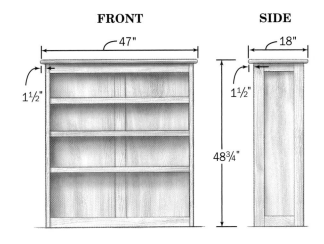

FRONT

47"

1½"

48¾"

SIDE

18"

1½"

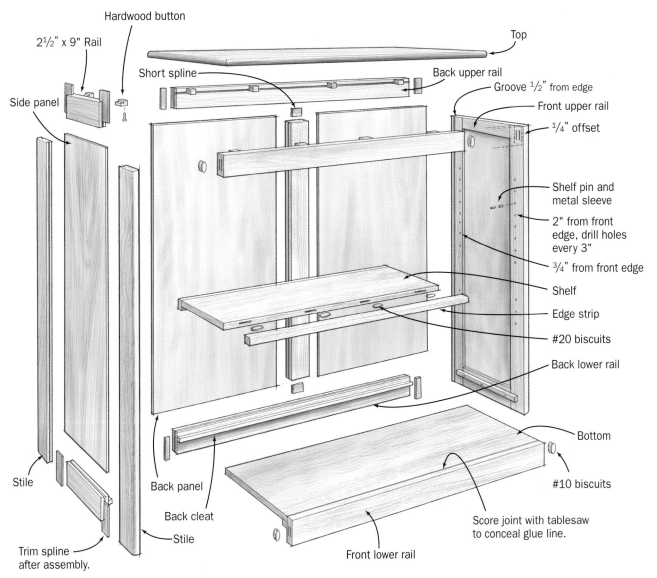

2½" x 9" Rail

Hardwood button

Short spline

Top

Back upper rail

Groove ½" from edge

Front upper rail

¼" offset

Side panel

Shelf pin and metal sleeve

2" from front edge, drill holes every 3"

¾" from front edge

Shelf

Edge strip

#20 biscuits

Back lower rail

Bottom

#10 biscuits

Back panel

Back cleat

Stile

Stile

Trim spline after assembly.

Front lower rail

Score joint with tablesaw to conceal glue line.

MATERIALS BOOKCASE

Quantity	Part	Actual Size	Notes
4	Stiles	1" x 3" x 48"	All wood is red oak (unless otherwise noted). To add legs like those on the sofa table, add 3" to length.
2	Front and back upper rails	1" x 2½" x 42"	
2 (1)	Front and back lower rails	1" x 3" x 42"	
2	Side rails (lower)	1" x 3" x 9"	
2	Side rails (upper)	1" x 2½" x 9"	
1	Back divider	1" x 2½" x 42½"	
12	Long splines	½" x 1" x varies	Thickness should be equal to panel thickness. Cut long and trim flush after assembly.
2	Short splines	½" x 1" x 1½"	Used to join ends of back divider to back rails
4	Back panels	¼" x 20¾" x 43½"	Oak plywood
4	Side panels	¼" x 10" x 43½"	Oak plywood
12	Hardwood buttons	¾" x 1½" x 2"	Walnut used here, but any straight-grained hardwood will do.
2	Front and back cleats	¾" x ¾" x 42"	
2	Side cleats	¾" x ¾" x 7½"	
1	Bottom	¾" x 12½" x 42"	Oak plywood
3	Shelves	¾" x 11½" x 42"	Cut a hair less than 42" to fit between sides.
6	Edge strips	1" x 1½" x 42"	Cut to match shelves.
1	Top	¾" x 18" x 47"	
24 (12)	1¼" #10 wood screws		
4	#0 biscuits		Use with upper front rail.
4	#10 biscuits		Use with lower front rail.
24	#20 biscuits		Use to align edging strips to shelves.
40	Metal sleeves		See Sources on p. 170.
12	Shelf pins		See Sources on p. 170.
	Yellow glue		Use with panels and biscuits.
	Polyurethane glue		Use when attaching splines.
1 quart	Stain		Stain is a good way to color-match the solid oak and oak plywood.
1 pint	Wipe-on polyurethane		
	Miscellaneous		150-grit, 180-grit, and 220-grit sanding discs (2 of each), cotton rags, wax *To build the hutch as shown on p. 126.

*Delete those parts indicated in bold and use quantities given in parentheses ( ).

Buying Materials

I used 5/4 oak (planed to 1" thick) to make the rails and stiles for aesthetic and practical reasons. The extra ¼" over traditional off-the-shelf lumber may not seem like much, but the extra thickness adds to the project's visual weight and sense of solidity in a big way. Similarly, the ½"-thick panels strengthen the case and provide the solid feel you'd expect from a well-built piece of furniture.

TOOLS

- Tape measure
- Tablesaw with rip blade and dado cutter
- Miter saw
- Two (preferably four) 50" panel clamps
- Biscuit jointer
- 12" combination square
- Block, #4, or #5 plane
- Card scraper
- Cabinet scraper
- Flush-cut saw
- Router
- ⅜"-diameter roundover bit
- Clamps
- ³⁄₁₆"-diameter drill and ⅜" countersink bits
- Drill
- Screwdriver
- Shelf sleeve-setting punch

Building the Bookcase

Abig project like this bookcase starts with a few simple cuts. To make the long boards easier to handle, it's best to cut the rails and stiles to rough length, arrange the pieces so that the grain looks good when the case is assembled, and then cut them to final dimension. The cutting and grooving sequence described here is similar to that used to build the sofa table in chapter 5. You may want to flip through that chapter for additional photos and tips.

You can also tweak the building process and combine this project with the sofa table (see the photo on p. 96) to make a handsome hutch. At first glance, this room-size project might seem too ambitious for a beginning woodworker, but look closer. You might be more than halfway there. To turn the bookcase into a hutch, refer back to the materials list on p. 120 and omit those parts listed in bold. If you wish, you may also reduce the width of the bookcase's edging from 1½" to 1" to match the lower shelf.

Two projects are better than one. You can build this contemporary hutch simply by combining the sofa table project with the bookcase. Use one or all three complementing pieces to solve your home storage shortage.

Cutting the Rails and Stiles to Size

1. Start by cutting the solid wood case parts to rough length—about an inch longer than the final dimensions in the materials list. To make the stiles, crosscut four boards to 49" long. Next, cut five boards to 43" long to make the front rails, back rails, and the center divider. To ensure the best grain match, cut the upper and lower side rails from a single 10"-long by 6"-wide board.

WORK SMART

It may look the same, but what was identified as a "leg" for the sofa table is referred to as a "stile" for the bookcase. (Similarly, dadoes and grooves become rabbets when milled along the end or edge of a board.) In frame-and-panel construction, rails run horizontally, stiles run vertically.

Like the sofa table, this project is easy to adapt. By changing a few of the overall dimensions, you can make a bookcase better suited to a room or make several different units to outfit an office or library. If you build the tower, you can edge the shelves with just a thin strip. Sagging won't be a problem over the short span of the shelves.

	Height	Width	Depth
Two-shelf	29"	51"	12"
Tower	72" to 96"	16"	12"

The size of the openings between shelves depends on several factors, and one of the most important is what you intend to store. These measurements may help you plan how many shelves you need.

Items on Shelf	Required Shelf Height
CDs/DVDs, videos, paperback books	7" to 8"
Hardcover books, magazines	10" to 12"
Tall books, display magazines	13" to 15"

Build your own library. Changing a few dimensions will dramatically transform the appearance, but not the construction sequence.

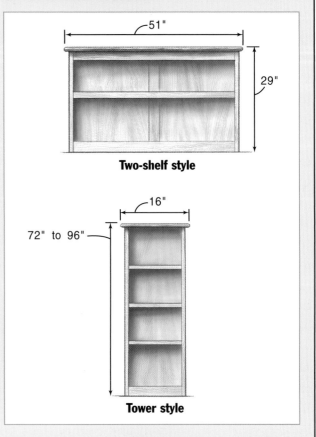

Two-shelf style

Tower style

2. Joint one edge of each board, then rip them to width. Set your fence and make all the same-size cuts at the same time. Rip the stiles and bottom rails to 3" wide. Reset your fence to 2½" and rip the top rails and center divider.

3. Crosscut the boards to final length. Cut the stiles to 48", the back divider to 42½", and the front and back rails to 42". The four side rails should be cut to 9".

4. Rout the outside corners of the stiles using your router table and a ⅜"-diameter roundover bit. Adjust the height of the bit and location of the fence to create the smoothest possible curve (without a bead or lipped

edge), then rout the stiles upright, on edge. If you to plan to build the hutch, mark the fence's location on your router table's base. By using the line to reposition the fence, you'll only need to fuss with the height of the bit.

WORK SMART

If you're working in a garage or basement shop, a few sheets of plywood can transform your cement floor into a serviceable ground-level worksurface. Shim the plywood as needed to make it as flat and level as possible. Seal the wood with polyurethane or remove it when it's not being used so that it doesn't wick up moisture from the cement.

Making the Plywood Panels

Even when it's full of books, you'll see a lot of the inside of this bookcase. It only makes sense to make the inside look as nice as the outside. To make a panel that doesn't have a bad side, you'll glue together two pieces of ¼"-thick plywood. The thicker panels also give a more solid feel to the case. You'll need about 1½ sheets of plywood. Make sure to inspect the plywood to be sure you're getting the best possible match.

Cutting plywood panels. **Crosscutting the back panels with an edge guide is a cinch.**

1. Cut the panels to rough dimension, then trim them to exact size when they're more manageable (refer to "Skill Builder: Cutting Plywood Down to Size" on pp. 104–105). Rip two 11" by 96" strips for the four side panels. Next, measure off the remaining factory edge and rip a 22"-wide strip to make two panels for the back. Rip another 22" strip off the second sheet to make the other two back panels. Crosscut the four strips in half to make eight 4'-long panels for the front and back as shown in the photo at right.

2. Arrange the plywood panels for the best grain match (inside and outside the case).

After deciding what parts go where, spread a thin coat of yellow glue onto the inside faces and lay the panels together. Trim the panels to final size after the glue dries.

3. Sand both faces of each panel up to 220 grit. Plane a light chamfer along the ends and edges of both side panels. Chamfering the edge will make the panels easier to fit into the grooves in the legs and rails and lessen the chance of catching an edge and splintering the face veneer during assembly. Stain the panels before assembly to ensure even color coverage. Otherwise, a small drop of dried glue can cause a major headache.

Grooving the Legs and Rails

Switch out your rip blade and install the inner- and outermost blades of your dado cutter. Grooving the rails and stiles in two passes may seem like it would take longer, but this two-pass method can save time in the long run. Cutting half the groove, then flipping the board end for end and cutting the second half guarantees that the groove is centered on the board without

needless fence adjustments. Because any movement to the fence is doubled by this "rip-and-flip" method, be careful when making adjustments to size the groove to the panel.

1. Install your dado cutter and attach a plywood auxiliary fence so that you have a wider bearing surface to guide the boards against as you run them on edge over your saw. Next, adjust the rip fence so that the cutter is roughly centered on the board. Using a piece of scrap, cut a ¼"-deep groove, then flip the board so that the opposite face is against the fence and make a second pass. Adjust the fence in small increments away from the blade until the ½"-thick panel fits snugly. To allow a little wiggle room during assembly, raise the cutter a hair above ½".

2. You're now ready to groove the inside edges of the stiles, the inside edges of the back rails, and both edges of the back divider. Do not groove the front rails; there's no panel in the front of the case.

3. Replace your auxiliary fence with your tenoning jig (refer to "Skill Builder: Cutting Tenons on the Tablesaw" on pp. 86–87.) Adjust the rip fence so that the groove along the end aligns with the edge grooves. Cut a

½"-wide centered groove on both ends of the four side rails, two back rails, and back divider using the two-pass method, just as you did along the edges.

4. The next step is to groove the back legs for the back panel. Note that the back rails are inset by ¼". To cut this groove, don't touch the dado height; just adjust your fence so that the groove starts ⅝" from the back edge. Cut the inside faces of both back legs, then adjust the fence to fit the two-ply panel and make a second pass.

5. The last step is to groove the top edge of the four upper rails for the wood buttons. Lower the cutter height to ⅜" and adjust the fence so that the groove starts ⅜" away from the top edge of the upper rail. Cut a ¼"-wide groove along the top edges of all four top rails, then adjust the fence to widen the groove to ⅜" and make a second pass.

Making a double-biscuit joint

1. Start with the stiles. Butt the two front stiles together so that the inside face is up, and use your combination square to mark the locations of the upper and lower rails. Find the midpoint and draw a reference line for your biscuit jointer.

To cut the double-biscuit slot with a ¼" offset, position the stile on your bench, front edge down. Place two ¼" spacers under the base of the mortise, align the cut line on the biscuit jointer with the reference line you made on the leg, and cut the first slot. Add a third spacer and cut the second slot. Repeat this same process with the other leg.

2. Draw centerlines on both ends of the upper and lower rails. Position the top rail

against your bench, outside face down, and set your biscuit jointer to #0. Place one spacer under the jointer and make the first cut. Next, add a second spacer and make the second cut. Set the depth adjustment to #10 before slotting the bottom rail.

Spacers make it simple. Use three ¼" spacers for the stile and two for rail. The ¼" hardboard scrap ensures even spacing and the ¼" offset.

Assembling the Panels

When gluing together a big assembly, you may want to enlist a helper and possibly invest in a few more clamps. Four 50" clamps would certainly be handy, but before you hit the hardware store, think about future projects. A pair of 60" clamps costs only a few dollars more than the slightly shorter clamps but will be handy for larger projects like the bed in chapter 7.

1. Before you start clamping things together, you'll need to cut spline stock. Set your rip fence to cut a strip as wide as the thickness of two pieces of ¼" plywood. Cut two 1½"-long splines for the back divider, but leave the rest longer. As you build each panel, you'll use what you cut off for the next assembly.

2. Assemble the side panels first. Apply glue to the grooves along the edges of the stiles and side rails. After clamping the side assembly and checking for square, spread a small amount of polyurethane glue on the long splines and slide one into the four grooves where the rails meet the stiles.

3. Before assembling the back panel, cut two 42½"-long spacer strips. Position the spacers at each end to ensure that the top rail stays parallel with the bottom. When clamping the back rails to the panels, be careful not to tighten the clamps too much, or you'll bow the spacers. The outside edges of panels should project from both ends of the rails by ½".

4. To assemble the case, start by placing one side assembly on a flat surface. Spread a thin bead of glue in the groove on the back stile and insert the back panel. Use a pair of

Slice it off. A flush-cut saw has no set to the teeth. This enables you to make a flush cut without scratching the surface. Clean up the cut with a plane.

squaring triangles (See "Jig: Squaring Triangle" on p. 67) to support this assembly as you glue and attach the opposite side panel. If you have enough clamps, go ahead and install the front rails. Apply polyurethane glue to the splines and insert them into the grooves where the sides meet the back.

5. As soon as the polyurethane foam isn't sticky, you can trim the splines. First, use a flush-cut or dovetail saw to remove most of the material, then finish up with a plane as shown in the photo above.

WORK SMART

A fresh razor blade, like the one in your utility knife, can be used as a scraper for removing glue stuck inside tight corners of assembled projects. Hold it at an angle and push or pull it with the grain of the wood.

Drop in the bottom

1. Use a combination square to establish a line ¾" down (the thickness of the bottom) from the top edge of the lower rails. Drill pilot and countersink holes into the cleats, then use the line on the rail as a guide as you attach them with 1¼"-long screws.

2. Cut the bottom so that it fits into the case. When you get a good fit, adjust your tablesaw to make a ¹⁄₁₆"-deep (or less) cut and score the top edges of the bottom panel.

Building Sturdy Shelves

Shelf building may not be an art, but it is an important woodworking skill to master. Besides looking good, shelves must be straight and sturdy. Bookcases in particular should be able to hold a full load of books or magazines without sagging. You can use your biscuit jointer and hardwood edging to make rock-solid plywood shelves quickly and easily. You'll also learn a fail-safe way to make those shelves wobble-free.

1. Use the materials list as a guide, but at this point, it makes more sense to measure the inside width of your case, then cut the shelves to fit. Cut them a hair shorter so that you can move them around. Next, rip six wood strips to 1½" to make the edge strips. Don't worry about cutting the boards to exact length; you'll trim the ends after they're glued to the plywood.

2. Arrange the edge strips on your bench, then use your combination square to make four evenly spaced lines across the boards. These will serve as the reference lines for your biscuit jointer. With the depth fence set to ¾", set the cutter to #20 and cut four slots in each strip as shown (see photo A).

3. Using one of the edge strips as a template, transfer the reference lines to both

A row of biscuits. Move the front piece to the back after cutting the four slots. Arranging the strips like this gives the biscuit jointer's fence a wide surface to lean on.

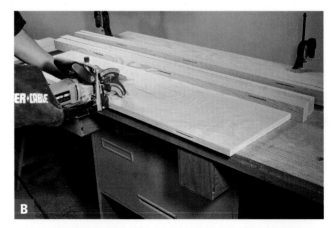

Slotting the shelves. Hang the shelf over the edge of your bench to ensure that the biscuit jointer rests on the fence, not on its base, as it cuts the slot.

Solid wood edging can do more than just hide the edges of plywood; it can also add a significant amount of strength to your shelf. Because heavy-duty edging isn't needed for every project, it helps to have a few choices for edging. The first two solutions can even be used to repair existing shelves. If you use matching wood, few will notice any difference.

Good: A thin wood strip adds a small amount of strength, but its main purpose is to cover up the plywood edge. Iron-on veneer tape is also available, but it offers little support. Tablesawn-ripped strips are easy to make and will match the rest of your project.

Better: Attaching a board edge to edge with the plywood adds more strength, but still main-

tains a thin profile. Adding a few biscuits adds some additional mechanical strength and prevents the wood from slipping when you clamp it up.

Best: Attaching a wide hardwood strip on its side to the edge of the shelf—either by fitting the plywood into a rabbet or with biscuits—can triple the strength of the shelf. Attach the wood so that the edge sticks above the top face of the plywood, then plane or scrape flush.

edges of the shelves. Once marked, use your biscuit jointer to cut four slots on both sides (see photo B).

4. Apply glue to the slots and sides, then clamp the strips to the sides. Arrange the shelves back to back to save clamps (see photo C).

5. Once dry, sand or scrape the top edge of the strip to bring it flush with the plywood (see photo D on p. 128). To avoid accidentally scraping or sanding through the veneer, draw pencil lines on the surface. Stop what you're doing the second those lines disappear.

Two shelves at once. Here's one way to work twice as fast with half as many clamps. Allow the glue at least an hour to dry before removing the clamps.

Scraper on steroids. Although it works like a regular card scraper, a cabinet scraper's plane-like sole leaves a flatter surface. Stop when the pencil lines disappear.

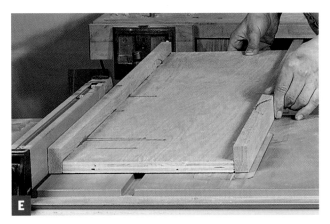

Notching makes it less noticeable. Cutting a shallow kerf to separate the edging from the plywood is easier on the eye than contrasting grain lines.

6. Sometimes the best way to conceal a joint is to draw attention to it. Adjust your rip fence to the position of the glue line and set the blade height to just scratch the surface of the wood, then score the top face of the shelves as shown (see photo E). If you like, you may rout the top edge of the shelf, or knock off the sharp corner with a block plane.

7. To prevent wobble, the holes for the shelf supports must be the same height in all four corners. To do this I used a simple drilling template made from a scrap of ¼" pegboard. After drilling the holes, use a punch to install the metal sleeves.

Building the Top

If you have extra 1"-thick material, feel free to make the top thicker than the dimensions given in the materials list, but since strength isn't an issue, I opted to save a little money by downsizing to ¾" stock. I also saved by making the top fasteners from walnut scrap that was gathering dust. (Refer to "Skill Builder: Making Tabletop Fasteners" on pp. 114–115.

Routing a Top in Two Steps

Step 1: Clamp top to bench and rout as shown.

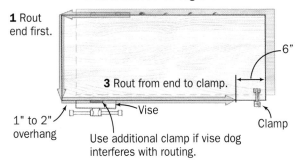

2 Rout from bench dog to end.

1 Rout end first.

6"

3 Rout from end to clamp.

1" to 2" overhang

Vise

Clamp

Use additional clamp if vise dog interferes with routing.

Step 2: Rotate top counterclockwise to finish routing opposite end and missed edges.

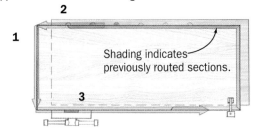

Shading indicates previously routed sections.

1. Rough-cut your boards to 50" (a little longer than you need to enable you to find a good grain match). Once in position, mark the boards, joint one edge, and glue up the top. When dry, rip the top to 18", then crosscut to 47". Sand both sides up 220 grit.

JIG: SHELF-DRILLING GUIDE

You can buy a shelf-drilling jig, but you can get by just fine with a scrap of ¼" pegboard. To make this jig, simply cut a strip of pegboard to fit inside your case. (Make sure the bottom edge is parallel to the rows of holes.)

Trim the edge of the pegboard to adjust the hole distance from either edge of the case. To ensure that the holes on both sides are the same distance from the front and back edges, draw a pair of arrows on the top of the jig and orient it so that the arrows always point toward the top and front of the case.

A simple shelf-pin guide of ¼"-thick pegboard is inexpensive, and more than accurate enough for this use. Cut a few strips to commonly used lengths, or rip a strip when it's needed.

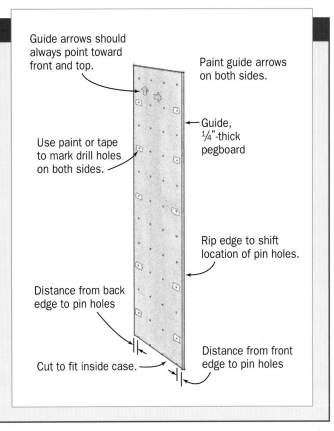

Guide arrows should always point toward front and top.

Paint guide arrows on both sides.

Use paint or tape to mark drill holes on both sides.

Guide, ¼"-thick pegboard

Rip edge to shift location of pin holes.

Distance from back edge to pin holes

Distance from front edge to pin holes

Cut to fit inside case.

---

2. You can finish the edges of the top however you like, but to match the sofa table, I used the two-step roundover profile described in "Making a Bullnose Edge" on p. 113. The trickiest part of this step might be finding a way to rout all the way around a top's edge

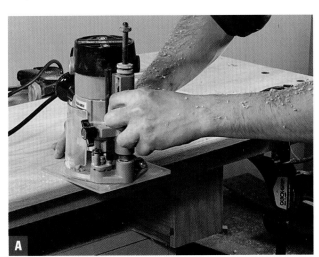

A

Three sides in one pass. Position your top so that you can rout the ends and a portion of the adjacent sides without having to stop and reposition interfering clamps or bench dogs.

without bumping into a clamp or bench dog. If you lay things out as shown in photo A, you will only need to reposition your top once.

3. Lay the top on top of the case so it overhangs the front, back, and sides by 1½" and clamp it in place. Drill pilot holes for the buttons, then fasten them to the top with 1¼" screws.

Finishing Touches

Apply one or two coats of wipe-on polyurethane to the interior and exterior surfaces. For a full-height bookcase, the top may not need additional protection. But if you're a plant lover, remove the top and brush on a coat or two of regular polyurethane to both sides. The extra protection will guard against damage from sweating pots and water overspill.

Simple Bed

When you begin shopping for a bed, you'll discover that commercial furniture makers are demanding premium prices for handcrafted details such as "eased corners," "hand-sanded surfaces," and "oil-and-wax finishes"—stuff you can do equally well in your shop. Isn't it time that you started making your own heirlooms instead of buying them at the mall?

Perhaps furniture stores are the ones responsible for starting the rumor that big projects are too difficult for beginning woodworkers in small shops—they don't want you to know that a big project like a bed can be boiled down into just a few simple parts: a headboard, a footboard, and a pair of rails to tie the two together. Once you understand the basic construction process, even making changes to fit your personal style isn't a big deal. In the following pages, you'll also learn ways to shrink the footboard, remove the slats, and even create a frame-and-panel footboard.

This bed was deliberately designed to fit into almost any bedroom. One way to do this is to take design cues from a few different styles. For example, the rectilinear slats and legs are in keeping with solid Arts and Crafts furniture, but the simple form, and the use of cherry instead of oak, evokes a lighter Shaker feel. Another way to make a project a universal fit is by designing it to complement existing decor without competing for attention. In that vein, this headboard and footboard were made slightly smaller than many Arts and Crafts beds so that they wouldn't overpower other pieces in a small room.

This project was built to accommodate both a mattress and a box spring, but these days you can get by with just a mattress. In that case, consider raising the ledger strips so that the support planks sit just below the top edge of the side rails.

What You'll Learn

- Handling big boards in a small shop
- Using epoxy to hide blemishes
- No-mortise mortise-and-tenon joinery
- Cutting wide dadoes with a router
- Using planes and chisels to make a finished surface

Make your own mark. Hand-cut details, like chamfered edges, add visual and tactile interest that you can't get from power tools.

Balancing acts with benchtop tools. Learn how to safely manage long boards on small saws by providing support before, during, and after the cut.

While beginning woodworkers will have an enjoyable time tackling this project, it offers plenty of opportunities to learn a few new things regardless of your level of expertise.

If you haven't been introduced to no-mortise bed-rail fasteners, you're in for a pleasant surprise. Instead of drilling holes through the legs for a bed bolt, or making a mortise for a metal hook, these fasteners simply screw to the legs and rails and rely on gravity to lock them together. These inexpensive fasteners are solid, yet easy to knock apart when it's time to move the bed.

In earlier chapters, you were introduced to mortise-and-tenon joinery. Here, you'll learn a technique for making the multiple mortises for the slats in the headboard and footboard without endless drilling or chiseling. Instead, you'll build a router jig designed to rout wide dadoes across one board, then cut the notched board into strips that fit into

A Flexible Bed Design

This bed is fine as is, but both the dimensions and the construction methods can be used as a template for making several different beds. Metal hardware and mortise strips simplify the trickiest construction steps.

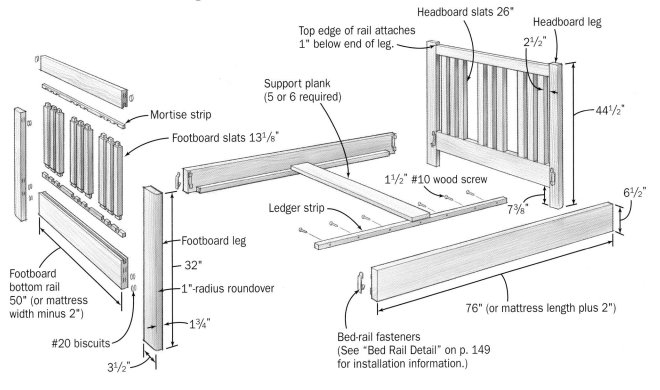

Top edge of rail attaches 1" below end of leg.

Headboard slats 26"

Headboard leg

2½"

44½"

Support plank (5 or 6 required)

Mortise strip

Footboard slats 13⅛"

1½" #10 wood screw

6½"

7⅜"

Ledger strip

Footboard leg

32"

1"-radius roundover

1¾"

Footboard bottom rail 50" (or mattress width minus 2")

#20 biscuits

3½"

Bed-rail fasteners (See "Bed Rail Detail" on p. 149 for installation information.)

76" (or mattress length plus 2")

---

headboard and footboard rails. Turning the dadoes into a ready-made mortise strip ensures tight-fitting slats and perfect top-to-bottom alignment.

Finally, you'll have an opportunity to fine-tune your plane and chisel skills as you finish the legs and rails. The chisel-chamfered legs and hand-planed surfaces may not appear as "perfect" as a piece that's pushed through a stroke sander, but when done well, the surface will gleam under a coat of oil. Once you've run your fingers over the tiny facets left on a hand-tooled surface, you may find that there's no going back.

Buying Materials

Building a bed requires fairly big boards. The legs and rails are made from 8/4 and 6/4 stock, respectively. If the milled wood is slightly thicker than what's listed in the materials list, stop while you're ahead—the added thickness will only add a little extra visual "weight" to your project. Just make sure that the boards used for the legs are all one thickness, and the material for the rails is about ¼" thinner.

MATERIALS

Quantity	Part	Actual Size	Notes
2	Side rails	1¼" x 6½" x 76"	6/4 hardwood. Don't worry if the two rails don't match perfectly; few people will ever see both at once.
2	Ledger strips	¾" x 1" x 73"	Use whatever hardwood stock you have on hand.
2	Headboard and footboard bottom rails	1¼" x 6½" x 50"	6/4 hardwood. Cherry, walnut, oak, or maple would all work well.
2	Headboard and footboard top rails	1¼" x 4½" x 50"	6/4 hardwood. Position the top and bottom rail stock next to each other (before cutting to length) to ensure a pleasing grain match.
2	Headboard legs	1¾" x 3½" x 44½"	8/4 hardwood. You probably want the legs to match the rails.
2	Footboard legs	1¾" x 3½" x 32"	8/4 hardwood
9	Headboard slats	¾" x 2¼" x 26"	Cherry was used here, but you can use a different species for a nice contrast. Cut a few extra to ensure good grain match from slat to slat.
9	Footboard slats	¾" x 2¼" x 13⅛"	Cut a few extra to ensure good grain match from slat to slat.
4	Mortise strips	9/16" x ½" x 50"	Cut strips 2" long and trim to fit after gluing into rails.
5 or 6	Support planks	¾" x 5½" x 52⅞"	Pine or poplar is fine. Space them evenly across the ledger strips to support the box spring.
24	Biscuits #20		Buy a container.
14	1½" #10 wood screws		To attach ledger strips to side rails
4	Bed-rail fasteners		See Sources on p. 170.
32	1" #8 wood screws		To attach bed hardware to side rails and legs
	Yellow glue		Extended or slower-setting glue can be handy for assembling head- and footboards.
1 pint	Oil/varnish finish		The tops of the legs will wick in oil like a sponge.
	Miscellaneous		Wax, blue masking (painter's) tape, white synthetic wool pad, cotton rags, 150- and 220-grit sandpaper (sheets and disks)

MATERIALS—SHORT-STYLE FOOTBOARD

Quantity	Part	Actual Size	Notes
2	Short legs	1¾" x 3½" x 15"	Two 8/4 short legs can be made with less material than it takes to make one headboard leg.
1	Footboard rail	1¼" x 6½" x 50"	
8	#20 Biscuits		

The mortises are cut as a strip from a piece of ½"-thick wood. If you don't yet own a planer, ask your mill operator to plane down an 8' board for you. (Ideally, the finished board should be about 9/16" thick; you'll plane it to exact thickness once it's glued in place.)

Assembling the headboard and footboard will require a pair of long clamps. One pair of 60" K-body clamps is a good investment, but if you already have pipe clamps, you can save money by buying an appropriately long piece of black pipe.

TOOLS

- Tape measure
- Tablesaw with rip blade and dado cutter
- Miter saw
- Biscuit jointer
- Drill press (optional)
- 12" combination square
- Block and #4 or #5 handplane
- ½" or ¾" chisel
- Card scraper
- Planer (optional)
- Router table
- 1"-radius roundover bit
- ½"-diameter straight bit
- Bearing-guided chamfer bit
- ⅛"-diameter drill bit
- ⅜"-diameter countersink bit
- 7/32"-diameter centering drill bit
- Drill
- Screwdriver
- Marking knife
- Marking gauge
- Two 60"-long bar clamps or two strap clamps
- Several small bar clamps
- Random-orbit sander

Building the Bed

As you cut the parts, "read" the wood and use it to its best advantage. For example, if a board has a minor bow, it can't be used for the headboard or footboard, but it might work well on the side rails. Arrange leg, rail, and slat boards so that the grain works in a way that's complementary, not conflicting.

Take time to finish before assembly. If the surface will be not be glued later on, apply a light coat of oil/varnish finish after you've planed or sanded it smooth. The finish will help protect the surface of the wood from fingerprints and glue drips and will point out any rough spots that you might have missed.

Start and Finish the Rails

As with the other projects, you'll cut the longest boards first. If you make a mistake, you'll still have a few big boards sitting around, and you may be able to salvage shorter pieces from your mistake.

1. Using the measurements from your mattress, cut the rails for the sides, headboard, and footboard to rough length. Normally, an extra inch is more than enough, but in this case, you'll want to cut one bottom and one top rail 4" to 6" longer than needed. (You'll use the cutoffs later as slot-spacing gauges when cutting the biscuit slots.)

2. Joint one edge, then set your tablesaw fence to 6½" and rip the side rails and the bottom rails for the headboard and footboard. (For tips on cutting long boards on benchtop tools, see "Skill Builder: Cutting Big Boards in a Small Shop" on p. 138.) Reset your fence to 4½" and rip the boards for the top rails. Place the headboard and footboard pieces safely aside for now.

WORK SMART

If your mattress is larger than "standard" dimensions, you won't be able to squeeze it into an undersized frame. Measure your mattress before cutting any stock and adjust your plans as necessary to fit your mattress. The frame's interior dimension should be 2" longer and 1" wider than the box spring or mattress.

3. Using your miter saw, or circular saw and edge guide, cut the side rails to length. The extra 2" allows some wiggle room for the mattress, so it's okay if you're off by as much as ¼". Just make sure that the rails are the same length.

4. Cut the ledger strips so that they are 3" shorter than your side rails. After cutting them to size, drill, countersink, and attach the cleats to the rails using 1½"-long screws, spaced about 1' apart. (Because I own a box spring, I attached the strips so that the

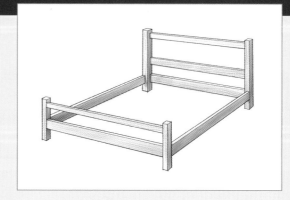

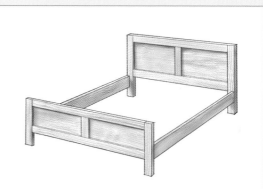

Using what you've learned from the first chapters of this book, you can adapt this plan to make several different styles of bed. Dimensions and photos are given for both tall and short footboards, but for a different look, you can also omit the slats in the head and/or footboard.

If you prefer the frame-and-panel style like the drawing shown at bottom right, groove the legs and end rails as described in chapter 6 on p. 106. Dry-assemble the frame to find the measurement of the center panel.

SLATLESS STYLE

Omitting the mortise strips and slats makes the bed look lighter and makes the project easier to build. You could build two twin-size frames to outfit a kids' room in a long weekend.

SOLID-PANEL STYLE

If you choose solid wood, widen the grooves in the legs and fasten the panel only in the center so that it's free to move across its width. Plywood panels eliminate the need to worry about wood movement.

---

bottom edge is flush with the bottom edge of the side rail. If you use only a mattress, consider raising the strips so that the top edge is 1" below the top edge of the side rail.)

5. Knock the sharp edges off the edges of the rails and ledger strips. The fastest way to do this is with a router and bearing-guided chamfer bit as shown in photo A, but a block plane will work just as well.

6. Lay both rails on your bench so that the ledger strips are facing up. Refer to the drawing on p. 149 to see how the hardware should be oriented, and lay pieces onto the

A

Better-balanced router. Unless chamfered, cherry and maple edges are sharp enough to slice skin. Balance the base of the router on scrap, as shown, when chamfering the outside edges.

ends so that you have a "left" and "right" side. Use a centering bit to drill pilot holes, then screw the metal clips in place (see photo B).

7. Before putting the rails aside, apply at least one coat of finish to protect them from glue and miscellaneous shop stains. Temporarily remove the hardware, plane and/or sand the rails up to 220-grit, then wipe on a coat of oil. Wait 20 minutes, then wipe away any excess. Apply at least three coats before top-coating with wax.

Quick clips. To ensure a gap-free connection, butt the side rails against a scrap of wood when attaching the bed-rail fasteners. That way, the metal edges can't extend past the end as you drive the screws.

Making the Legs

From a distance, the legs may appear massive, but they're only 1¾" thick—about the same thickness as standard 2-by lumber. Thick, square posts would add a more substantial look, but they won't make the bed any sturdier. Another consideration is price. The board foot price of 16/4 stock is usually more than twice the cost of 8/4 wood and isn't always available in all species.

To soften the outside corners, I used a roundover bit with a 1" radius. Large-diameter bits should only be used with larger (2 hp or more) routers that can be slowed down to a safe cutting speed. If you don't feel like springing for a big bit, or don't yet own a router with speed control, you can knock off corners with a smaller bit or cut the bevel with your tablesaw, as shown in photo B on p. 139, then use your block plane to finish the roundover process.

1. Start by cutting the legs to rough length (cut the headboard legs to about 46" and the footboard legs to about 33"). Joint one edge, then set your tablesaw to 3½" and rip all four pieces to width. Now that they're a more

WORK SMART

Inspect both edges and ends of each board before cutting to final dimension. This is your chance to cut off natural defects or tearout, blade burns, and snipe marks left by your planer or other machines.

manageable size, trim the headboard legs to 44½" and the footboard legs to 32".

2. Take a minute to decide how the legs will be oriented in relation to the bed. When you're happy with the way things look, use a pencil to mark the top end and the outside corner that you will round over. Next, position the legs on your bench so that the bottoms are against a straightedge and the inside edges face up, as shown in photo A on p. 139. Using a combination square, lay out the locations of the bottom and top rails.

3. To produce a smoother corner and save your bit from needless wear and tear, use your tablesaw to remove some material from the

What You'll Need

- **Benchtop tablesaw**
- **Miter saw**
- **Roller stand (weighted down with sand)**
- **Bench-mounted roller supports**

One reason small-shop woodworkers stick with small projects is that they're uncomfortable wrestling big boards in a small space. Benchtop tools have the horsepower to make most cuts, but lacking the mass and footprint of larger machines, they may not be able to safely support the workpiece. Boards that topple off tools in midcut can result in damage to the work, machine, or both. But if you plan out your cuts and provide support at both ends of each board, your wood won't know whether you're working in an aircraft hangar or one-car garage.

SAFE, SUPPORTED RIPS

When ripping long boards on a benchtop tablesaw, a roller stand is a necessity for making smooth, safe cuts. Set the stand height so that it's about ⅛" below the saw table to prevent the board from catching the front edge. Position the stand close enough to your saw so it provides support before the board begins to tip off your saw, but far enough so that the board won't tip off the stand at the end of the cut. To provide extra stability, weigh down the stand's legs with a bag of sand, as shown (see photo A).

CONTROLLED CROSSCUTS

A miter saw can't cut accurately if the board tips or slips midcut. The saw's hold-downs

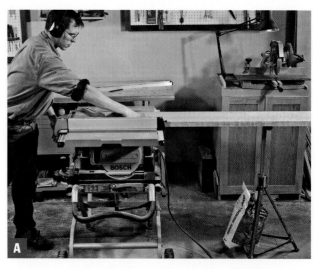

Better balanced board. Position the stand far enough away from the saw so that the board doesn't tip at the end of the cut. The sandbag ensures that the stand doesn't tip in midcut.

Double-duty workbench. Quick-clamping roller supports grab on to your bench or a sawhorse to support oversize stock. Use a 4' level to set the supports to the same level as the saw.

help, but for really long boards, an auxiliary table or fence is a better bet. The supports shown in photo B can be clamped onto any sawhorse or tabletop. Alternately, you can build a riser box that can sit on your bench, to support long boards.

Laying out the legs. Position the legs on your bench, inside face up, and mark the locations for the top and bottom rails. Use a scrap piece of rail stock to lay out the rail's location on the legs' inside edges.

corner first, as shown in photo B. Before you cut the legs, test-cut and rout a piece of scrap to be sure you're not sawing off too much wood.

4. Using your router table and 1" radius bit, round over the outside edge of each leg as shown in photo C on p. 140. Lower the operating speed of your router to prevent damaging you, your router, or your workpiece. (See "Safe Speeds for Big Bits" on p. 139.)

5. After softening the outside corner, knock down the remaining three sharp edges with a chamfer bit set just below ⅛" high, as shown in photo D on p. 140. (If you haven't already done so, this is a good excuse to build the vise-mounted router table described in "Skill Builder: Router Table" on pp. 28–29. This simple fixture will earn its keep when it's time to chamfer the edges on the 18 slats.)

6. Now for the fun part. Clamp one leg to your bench, as shown in photo A on p. 141. Using one or more of your favorite planes, knock down any bump that might exist at the edge of the rounded-over corner. Concentrate on knocking off any ridges along the corner to make the fairest curve possible. If your planes are working to your satisfaction, continue smoothing the outside faces of the

Precut corners. Instead of overworking your router, or wasting time repositioning the bit or fence to make multiple cuts, set your tablesaw to 45° and slice off the outside corner before routing.

C

Chew slowly and take small bites. Don't think big bits can remove all that wood at once. To prevent damage to the bit or board, take light cuts and slow down the router to a safer, slower speed.

leg. Alternately, you can hand-sand or use a random-orbit sander to smooth the legs up to 220 grit.

7. You no longer need the pencil marks on the tops of the legs to know which end goes up. Sand, plane, or slice off the reference marks you made earlier (no one will know if your leg is $^1/_{32}$" shorter than the given dimension). Next, secure the leg to your bench, bottom end up. At this point, you're ready to chamfer the ends. The chamfer on the bottom end prevents the wood from catching and splintering; on the top, it's purely for decoration.

Cutting a chamfer with a chisel is easier than you might think. Start by making short, light cuts. Resist the chisel's inclination to drive itself too deeply into the wood. Aim for about a $^1/_8$"-high chamfer as shown in photo B on the facing page, but feel free to stop when it looks good. After chamfering the bottoms of

D

Chamfer corners before they cut you. Armed with a bearing-guided bit, this simple router table is a champ at cutting light chamfers. Use it to soften the sharp edges from the legs, rails, and slats.

all four legs, sharpen your chisel and do the top ends. (Alternately, you can make the chamfer using a file or sandpaper wrapped around a block of wood.)

The speed at which a router bit turns can be important. The typical router runs at about 22,000 rpm, which is fine for most bits. But as the diameter of the bit increases, you'll want to slow things down. In the worst-case scenario, a big bit at full speed could spin itself apart. Before that happened, the bit would begin to flutter, which would cause even a brand-new bit to leave burnt edges or a rippled finish.

When using big bits, decreasing router speed can make routing safer and improve the quality of the cut. Below is a chart showing recommended speeds for various sizes of bits. If you find yourself burning edges with fresh bits, you may choose to use a speed slower than what's listed below. To be extra safe, big bits should be used only in a router table.

Bit Diameter	Recommended rpm
1" or less	Full speed
1" to 1½"	18,000
1½" to 2½"	15,000
More than 2½"	10,000

Making the Headboard and Footboard

Headboard and footboard rails usually rely on tenons to attach them to the legs. Tenons are a good choice; they're solid enough to help keep the frame square and can be designed to allow single-plank headboards room to move in response to changes in humidity. Sometimes, however, you can achieve the same effect with a simpler approach. In this case, biscuits make a perfectly serviceable joint; the narrow rails can be glued tight to the legs because they don't move as much as a wide panel headboard. Since the rails transfer the weight of the mattress directly to the leg, strength isn't a concern.

Plane around the corner. Set your blade to take light cuts, and focus on knocking off the ridge between the roundover and the flat face. The rounded edge will look smooth, but your fingertips will feel the facets on the legs.

Chiseled chamfers. Chiseling the chamfers on the ends not only eliminates the chance of burning or tearout, it also adds another interesting hand-tooled detail.

Starting the rails and finishing the slats

1. Pull out the headboard and footboard rails you made at the beginning of this project and cut all four boards 2" shorter than the width of your mattress or box spring (the width of the legs makes up for the 2" that the rails come up short). Next, lay them out on your bench and pick out the best faces of each and arrange them to make the most attractive pairs. (You may want to mark the rails to make sure they don't get switched around.) Knots or other blemishes can usually be hidden simply by flipping the board, but if there's a blemish that you can't work or cut around, refer to "Skill Builder: Hiding Knots and Blemishes," on p. 144 to learn how to make a near-invisible patch.

2. Temporarily put the rails aside and start cutting the slats. To make the slats, begin by cutting the ¾"-thick wood to rough length. (Rather than cutting the boards to two different lengths at this point, cut all the slat stock 27" long. From that length, you can make one headboard slat or two footboard slats. Cut two or three more than you need, just in case.) Joint one edge, then set your tablesaw to 2¼" and rip the strips to final width.

3. Using your router and chamfer bit set to ⅛" high, or just your block plane, chamfer the long edges of the four rails and your slat stock.

4. It's easier to sand and finish the slats now, rather than attempt to work between them once they're joined to the rails. Finish-sand all surfaces up to 220 grit, then apply one or two coats of oil.

5. While you're waiting for the oil to dry, focus your attention on the rails. Replace

Ready the rails for mortise strips. The mortise strips fit into a ½"-wide by ½"-deep groove. Use an auxiliary fence and featherboard at the tablesaw to prevent the rail from tipping in midcut.

your sawblade with the inner and outer blades from your dado cutter and set the cutter height to ½". Cut a ½"-wide groove centered along the bottom edge of the top rail and the top edge of the bottom rail. Start by making one pass, then turning the board end for end and cutting a second pass (see photo C). (Don't lose any sleep if the groove isn't exactly ½" wide; because the mortise strips are cut to fit, you can still get a tight-fitting joint.)

D

Cut the slats to size. By clamping a long-arm stop to your saw, you can be sure that all your slats are the same length. Cut a few extra before adjusting or removing the stop.

E

F

Slip-fit stub tenons. Starting with a test slat, use your tablesaw and dado cutter to nibble away at both sides of the tenon until it fits the groove. Adjust the cutter height so that the tenon doesn't wiggle from side to side.

6. When cutting the long and short slats to length, take a minute to set up a stop block system, like the setup shown in photo D, to ensure that your slats are cut to the same length. Before moving or removing the jig, cut two or three extra long and short slats, just in case you make a mistake later on in the assembly process.

7. Adjust the dado cutter so that it's just ⅛" high and ¼" away from the fence. Next, using your miter gauge to guide a sample slat, cut a tenon on one end as shown in photo E. If necessary, you can adjust the fit by changing the cutter height. Once you've gotten a good slip fit as shown in photo F, don't touch your saw's settings until you've finished tenoning all your slats.

What You'll Need

■ **Plastic cup and knife**

■ **5-minute epoxy**

■ **Sawdust**

■ **Chisel or card scraper**

With wood, cracks, checks, and knot holes are par for the course. It's usually best to work around defects and dents, but when that's not an option, try using this epoxy and sawdust filler. Using sawdust from the wood you're repairing guarantees a close color match. Epoxy can be machined like the surrounding wood, and it works under most finishes. Even under a clear finish, the patch resembles a hard knot.

1. Follow the instructions on the epoxy to mix the resin and hardener. As you mix, blend in some fine sawdust (the type you'd shake out of your sander after using 120- or 220-grit paper). Aim for a thick peanut-butter-like consistency (see photo A).

2. Once the patch is mixed, use your plastic knife to smear it into the cavity or crack (see photo B). Since you'll scrape away the excess, it's OK to apply more than what's needed. Try to avoid creating any bubbles or air pockets.

3. Using a card scraper, scrape the patch and the surrounding surface of the wood (see photo C). When the patch is flat, finish-sand the entire surface to conceal your work, and apply a finish.

B

Fill 'er up. Using a plastic knife, drip and spread the mix into the hole. Work quickly, or your patch may cure in the cup.

A

Making it match. You can make a matching patch with some sawdust and some 5-minute epoxy. Using the scraper to spoon in the sawdust, make the mix as thick as possible, but not crumbly.

C

Scrapes smooth, just like wood. When the patch has fully cured, a card scraper is used to smooth it out. Once flush, finish-sand the board and you're done.

Making mortise strips

The mortise strip starts out as a 4½" by 52" board dadoed across its top face, then ripped into strips that fit into the grooves cut into the headboard and footboard rails. Making four rows of "mortises" at once is faster than cutting them separately, and it ensures that the holes in the top and bottom rails line up.

1. Start by cutting the mortise board to rough size. Plane or resaw a board to ⁹⁄₁₆". Cut the board to 52" long (2" longer than your headboard and footboard rails). Draw lines at each end of the board to indicate the final length.

2. Use a 2½"-wide scrap spacer and one of the actual slats to lay out the dadoes. Center the first dado at the midpoint between your two pencil lines. Using the spacer board as a guide, start the second and third dado 2½" away from the center dado (on either side of the center dado). After laying out the three center slats, use the spacer to position the

first end slat 2½" in from the pencil line, and a slat to obtain the exact width of the dado. X out the dadoes as shown in photo G to ensure that you don't accidentally rout out "good" wood.

3. After marking out the board, the next step is to cut the dadoes with either your tablesaw or router. If you decide to try the router as shown in photo H, use the jig described in "Skill Builder: Routing Wide Dadoes" on p. 146.

4. To turn those dadoes into mortises, adjust the bevel angle of your tablesaw to 3°, then set your tablesaw's fence to rip a strip a hair thicker than the groove you made in the rail. When you rip the dadoed board, orient it so that the notched side is wider than the unnotched side.

5. In theory, the strip should fit into its groove like a cork in a bottle, but it's OK if you don't have a perfect fit yet. If it's too tight—either

Numberless layout. Use a 2½" spacer strip and your test slat to lay out the location of the dadoes on your mortise strip. Use your square to extend the lines, not to measure.

Mortises made easy. Make the "mortises" for all four rails at once by using your router and the wide dado jig.

What You'll Need

- Router with straight bit
- Four strips of plywood, ¾" by 3" by 12"
- 12" combination square
- Ten 1¼" deck screws
- Two or three 6" bar clamps

With four scraps of plywood and a handful of drywall screws, you can make a jig to cut any width of dado you need. When clamped against the board, this simple setup makes identically sized dadoes that are always square to the edge.

1. Cut the plywood strips first. Making the fences longer than the board helps guide the router's base at the beginning and end.

2. Attach the right-hand fence. Insert one screw, then use a combination square to make certain that the assembly is square before driving the other two screws.

You're ready to rout. Use the fences as guides to rout the sides of the dado, then remove the center section of the dado freehand.

Wide Dado-Routing Jig

This setup works with any router and straight bit combination.

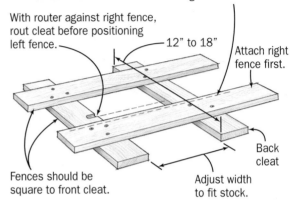

For consistent-width dadoes, mark fence and router so same side of router is used against fence.

With router against right fence, rout cleat before positioning left fence.

12" to 18"

Attach right fence first.

Fences should be square to front cleat.

Back cleat

Adjust width to fit stock.

3. Clamp the partially assembled jig to your bench, adjust your router to make a ⅛"-deep cut, and make a test cut on your front cleat. (Mark the fence and router to ensure that the same side of the router is used against the same fence. Not all router bases are perfectly symmetrical; changing the orientation can affect the width of the dado.)

4. Raise the bit above the surface of the board to help position your left-hand fence. If the cut and layout lines match up, attach the back cleat.

5. Work so that the bit's rotation keeps the router against your fences. Place the router against the right fence on the far side of the board and pull the router toward you. When the bit reaches the front cleat, slide the router to the left fence and push it back through the board. Remove the material in the middle of the dado with back-and-forth passes as shown.

Planed to perfection. Don't try to get a perfect-fitting strip straight off the tablesaw. Rip the strip slightly wider than you need, then plane to fit.

Shave away the evidence. To remove remaining blade marks and glue stains, plane the strip flush with the rail. Don't get carried away; stop planing as soon as your blade starts shaving the rail.

across the entire strip or just in a few spots—plane down one edge, as shown in photo I, until the strip fits with just a light mallet tap. Make sure to align the end marks on the notched strip. Use as little glue as possible; you don't want squeeze-out to fill your brand-new mortises.

6. The mortise strip was made 1/16" thicker than the depth of the groove. Use a hand-plane to trim the strip flush with the edge of the rail (see photo J). Set your plane for a light cut and balance it on the exposed strip. Stop planing as soon as the blade bites into the rail.

Assembling the headboard and footboard

1. Before you can start pulling the headboard and footboard together, you'll need to cut biscuit slots in the legs and end rails. Start by cutting a pair of biscuit slots in a scrap of 6½"-wide rail to see how far you can space the slots without coming out though the edges. Then transfer the slot locations to the leg stock as shown in photo K on p. 148. Continue laying out the slot locations to the bottoms of all four legs and both ends of the bottom ends of both end rails. Repeat this step using the 4½"-wide rail scrap to position the slots for the top rail.

2. The rails are offset from the legs by ¼". To offset the biscuit slots, place a leg flat-side down against your bench, lay one ¼" spacer

under your biscuit jointer, and cut the bottom slot. Insert two more ¼" spacers under the jointer and cut the higher slot as shown in photo L on p. 148. Repeat on all four legs.

3. To cut the slots in the rails, place the rail against your bench, inside face down, and cut the biscuit slots, first with no spacer, then with two, as shown in photo M on p. 148. When the rails are fit against the legs, their biscuit slots will be offset ¼" in from the edge of the leg. Repeat the biscuit-cutting process on all four rails.

4. You're now set to assemble the headboard and footboard. Assembling this many pieces at one time can be tricky, so try a dry run

Lay out the biscuit slots. Using a scrap piece of the bed's rail as a template (instead of reading numbers off your combination square) is a good way to avoid measurement-related errors.

without glue. This may also be a good time to enlist an extra pair of hands to assist with positioning the slats as you clamp things together.

Glue the slats into the rails, then glue the rails to the legs, using as many clamps as necessary to pull it all together and check for square (see photo N). When clamping, it's okay if the top rail shifts down slightly, but make sure the bottom rail doesn't move from your original layout lines.

5. Give the glue at least an hour before removing the clamps. You should allow the glue at least a full day to completely cure, but at this point you can remove any drips, finish-sand the legs, and coat unfinished surfaces with a coat of oil. After two or three coats of oil, apply a coat of wax to all finished surfaces and buff to a shine.

Slotting the legs. Starting with the inside face of your leg resting on your bench, use one ¼"-thick spacer to position the first biscuit slot and three to cut the second.

Slotting the rails. Place the rail on your bench, inside face down. With the biscuit jointer also resting on your bench, cut the first slot, then use two ¼"-thick spacers to cut the second.

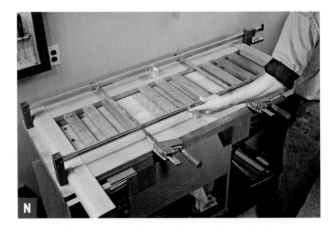

Clamp it tight. The blue tape is used to make sure the carefully arranged slats weren't shuffled during glue-up. Put blocks under the long bars to prevent them from bowing as the clamps are tightened.

Making the Bed

You're only a few screws and a couple of cuts away from finishing this project. Now's the time to be extra careful. An old joke claims that mistakes happen "when you start to smell the finish," but there's nothing funny about stripping or snapping that last screw, or dinging up a footboard because you were too impatient to ask someone to hold open a door.

1. Mount the bed-rail fasteners to the headboard and footboard legs as shown in the drawing at right. (If you're not using the same hardware, position the piece so that the side rails attach to the legs at the same height as the bottom rail of the headboard and footboard.) Use a centering bit to drill the pilot holes, then attach the metal clips using 1" #8 wood screws.

2. Attach the side rails to the headboard. If everything was installed correctly, the two should clip together as shown in photo A. Be careful not to twist the rails around too much at this point. The fasteners are strong enough to support the weight of the mattress and sleeper, but they can be damaged by levering the rail from side to side.

A

Simple assembly. The hardware on the side rails locks into place on the legs as it's dropped into place. At this point, be careful not to twist the frame (or you could damage the fastener).

Bed Rail Detail

Metal fasteners simplify assembly, but they should be installed precisely so that the bottom rails line up. Take a minute to see how the fasteners hook together before you start screwing them to the legs and side rails.

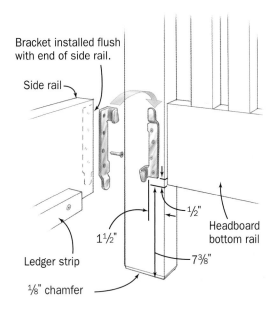

Bracket installed flush with end of side rail.

Side rail

Ledger strip

$\frac{1}{8}$" chamfer

$1\frac{1}{2}$"

$\frac{1}{2}$"

Headboard bottom rail

$7\frac{3}{8}$"

3. Cut the support planks about $\frac{1}{8}$" shorter than the distance between the side rails. The materials list specifies five or six planks, but if you're going without a box spring, you may need a few more. Alternately, if you install enough planks so that there is less than a 1" gap between boards, you can use a softer futon-like mattress.

4. Complete the bed with a box spring, mattress, mattress pad, linens, and comfy pillows, and it's ready for a well-deserved rest. You probably are too.

Desk

A comfortable desk is as essential to an efficient home office as your workbench is to your workshop. This project is designed to fit that bill. This desk provides plenty of space for studying, paying bills, or sketching out your next shop project. Plus, the drawers offer a built-in storage solution for keeping papers and essential office supplies out of sight until they're needed.

Although originally designed as a desk, this project is versatile enough to become a valuable worksurface almost anywhere in your home. With a few small changes to the base and/or top, you can turn this desk into a table that could complement most kitchen or family-room decor. A far more attractive and permanent alternative to the veritable card table, this project is suitable for casual chores such as doing homework and playing board games, but also elegant enough to serve as an extra dining table when company arrives.

Aside from the utility provided by the table itself, this project offers a valuable introduction to the process of table construction. (To fully appreciate the value of this lesson, take a minute to count how many tables are now in your home.) After building this desk, you'll have the skills you need to build future tables of your own creation. You'll learn how easy it is to adapt this design to create custom tables perfectly suited for their intended use and allotted space. For example, you could shrink these plans to build a 21" by 42" child's desk. On the other extreme, you could enlarge the top's dimensions to 36" by 72" and omit the drawers for a dining table to comfortably serve six.

What You'll Learn

- **Loose-tenon joinery**
- **Template mortising with a router**
- **Making a locking-rabbet drawer joint**
- **Working with aniline dyes**

This project was designed to be a useful addition to your home and to provide several important woodworking lessons that can be applied to future projects—regardless of their size or complexity.

In previous chapters, you've used your router for shaping and simple joinery. This chapter offers an introduction to bushing-guided template routing. The bushing, or collar, attaches to the base of the router. Creating a template for the bushing to ride against requires a little time, but once it's built, you'll get lots of use out of it in the future. Simply reattach the bushing and double-check the cutting depth of your bit, and you can rout a hundred mortises just as accurately as the first. You'll appreciate this technique when you rout the eight mortises used to attach the aprons to the legs, and another eight mortises to secure the top to the base.

The desk organizer and blanket box in earlier chapters offered simple drawer joinery techniques, but the desk drawer requires a more substantial solution. You'll learn how to cut a locking miter joint using your tablesaw and router table. Unlike a plain rabbet joint, the parts hook together to pull the drawer tight even before you drive nails or crack open a bottle of glue.

Mixing your own dye stains. Aniline dyes can add a little or a lot of color without masking the grain or texture of the wood. But there's a little more to using them than "just adding water."

Taming template mortising. Learn how to turn your router into an accurate mortising machine. All you need are a few guide bushings and some small pieces of acrylic or plywood.

Write This Way

Sized to fit most home offices, this desk can be made smaller to fit into a child's room or enlarged to serve as a casual dining table. The drawer's rear compartment keeps the drawer from tilting out when accessing the main space. To find this "secret" space, you'll need to pull the drawer completely out of its opening.

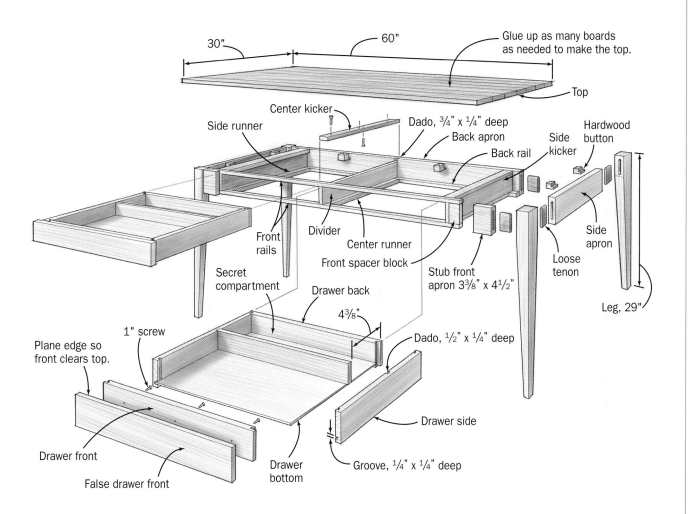

30"

60"

Glue up as many boards as needed to make the top.

Top

Center kicker

Side runner

Dado, ¾" x ¼" deep

Back apron

Back rail

Side kicker

Hardwood button

Front rails

Divider

Center runner

Front spacer block

Stub front apron 3⅜" x 4½"

Side apron

Loose tenon

Leg, 29"

Secret compartment

Drawer back

4⅜"

Dado, ½" x ¼" deep

1" screw

Plane edge so front clears top.

Drawer front

False drawer front

Drawer bottom

Groove, ¼" x ¼" deep

Drawer side

Buying Materials

When designing this project, I spied a pile of 4/4 curly maple hiding in the corner of the lumberyard. Depending on your lumber supplier, figured boards may cost a few dollars more. Less dramatic, straight-grained hard, or "rock," maple would look almost as nice, as would white or red oak. You may also choose a soft hardwood, like birch, or even a softwood such as pine—just be sure to invest in a writing pad to prevent scratching the desktop.

The aprons and drawers are made of soft maple. Soft maple is easier to plane and generally less expensive than the hard stuff,

Quantity	Part	Actual Size	Notes
1	Top	¾" x 30" x 60"	Hard maple, or comparable hardwood, is a good choice. You want the top to look good years from now.
4	Legs	2¼" x 2¼" x 29"	See Sources on p. 170.
2	Side aprons	¾" x 4½" x 21½"	Soft maple is a good choice for the base. It's easier to work with and less expensive than hard maple.
1	Back aprons	¾" x 4½" x 46"	
1	Back rail	¾" x ½" x 46"	
2	Stub front aprons	¾" x 4½" x 3⅜"	
2	False drawer fronts	¾" x 4½" x 19½"	Plane or rip 1⁄16" from top edge to clear bottom of tabletop.
2	Front rails	¾" x ½" x 46"	
2	Front spacer blocks	¾" x 3½" x 3"	
8	Loose tenons	5⁄16" x 3¼" x 2¼"	Make from leftover scraps of soft maple.
2	Side kickers	½" x 1½" x 23½"	
1	Center kicker	½" x 2½" x 23½"	
2	Side runners	½" x 1½" x 22¼"	
1	Center runner	½" x 2½" x 22¼"	
3	Dividers	¾" x 3½" x 24½"	
4	Drawer sides	½" x 3½" x 23"	
4	Drawer fronts and backs	½" x 3½" x 18¾"	Make sure fronts and backs fit into the front frame.
2	Drawer false backs	½" x 3" x 18¼"	
2	Drawer bottoms	¼" x 18¼" x 22¾"	Birch plywood
8	Hardwood buttons	¾" x 1½" x 2"	Walnut used here, but any straight-grained hardwood scrap will do.
26	1¼" #10 wood screws		To assemble drawer guides and attach buttons
7	1" #10 wood screws		To attach drawer to false front and kickers to tabletop
1 pint	Wiping varnish		For finishing top and sealing painted base
1 pint	Milk paint		See Sources on p. 170
	Miscellaneous		80-, 100-, 150-, 180-, and 220-grit paper (2 or more disks of each depending on condition of top); yellow glue; cotton rags; wax; 2" foam brush; cheesecloth; maroon abrasive pad; 000 steel wool

which should free up some assembly time and extra funds for a nicer top.

If you don't yet own a jointer and planer, ordering the 2¼" tapered legs (see Sources, on p. 170) may be the best way to approach this project. Ordering the legs also provides additional design options. Substituting a turned or cabriole-shaped leg instead of the Hepplewhite-style leg used here would change the look of the table, but not the construction sequence.

- Tape measure
- Tablesaw with rip blade
- Single blade from a stack dado cutter
- Miter saw
- 12" combination square
- Block and #4 or #5 handplane
- Card scraper
- Cabinet scraper or scraper plane
- File and burnisher
- Plunge router
- 7⁄16" and ½" (outside diameter) router bushings
- Chamfer bit
- ¼"-diameter spiral upcut router bit
- ⅛"-diameter straight bit
- 24"- and 50"-long panel clamps (preferably two of each)
- ⅛"- and ⅝"-diameter drill bits
- Countersink bit
- Drill
- Screwdriver
- Random-orbit sander

Building the Desk

Like the earlier projects, the desk can be broken down into bite-size subassemblies: the top, the base, and the drawers. You can start with either the top or the base, but don't cut drawer parts until you have an opening to fit them into. (I generally prefer to build the top first. This way, I'm sure to use the best boards where they'll be most visible.)

For a simpler table, you may choose to omit the drawers. In that case, make two aprons just like the back apron shown in the drawing on p. 153, instead of the short apron stubs and false drawer fronts. You'll still want to rout a single dado in both aprons for a center divider. Even though it doesn't support a drawer, the divider reinforces the base and provides an additional fastening point for the top.

Making the Top

One of the biggest advantages to building this desk yourself is that you're able to build it to fit your room. Since the top also establishes the "footprint" of this project, you can bring it inside, prop it on top of a pair of chairs or sawhorses, and make sure that it fits where it's intended to go.

Although finishing is always relegated to the end of the chapter, you might want to consider flipping a few pages ahead and finishing the top completely before starting the base and drawers. Staining and sealing the top is a good way to protect it from potential shop stains and will reduce its ability to absorb moisture from the air. If the weather conditions are right, your top could start bowing after just a weekend in an unheated shop.

1. Start by rough-cutting enough wood to make a solid panel a few inches wider and longer than your top's finished dimensions (in this case, 30" by 60"). Cutting the boards a little longer than you need will allow you to slide them around a little in order to get the best possible match. When in position, mark the boards, joint the edges, and glue up the top.

DESIGN OPTIONS

Table legs do more than support the top; they also establish the look of a project. That said, you can create tables of dramatically different styles simply by swapping out the legs for a different set. For example, using thick cabriole legs, like those shown in the photo at right, transforms the straight-lined desk into a more elegant dining table. To further customize your work, experiment with different tabletop edge and corner treatments.

Cabinet shops usually rely on wide-belt panel sanders called "time-savers" to flatten wide panels without leaving tearout. They're called time-savers for a reason, and most cabinet shops will run your tabletop through them for a small fee. Make a few calls, then weigh the cost against the time it would take you to do all the work yourself.

2. Allow the panel to dry for at least 24 hours before scraping off dried glue and finish sanding. Although yellow glue cures in a few hours, you'll want to be sure that the glue lines have released the moisture they absorbed from the glue. If you sand too soon, your panel will look flat at first, but as the wood dries, valleys will appear along the glue lines.

If you've selected figured wood for the top, neither the planer at the mill nor the one in your garage may be able to plane it to width without causing a lot of surface tearout. If that's the case, leave the boards about ⅛" thicker than final width, then use your scraper to remove any tearout and bring the panel to final thickness (see photo A). Finish up by power sanding. Expect to start as coarse as 80-grit to remove scratches and track marks. A plainer-grained top may require a similar scraping and sanding treatment to smooth out ridges where one board meets the next, although it shouldn't take nearly as long to produce a finished surface.

3. Unless you have a large auxiliary table, this top is too unwieldy to cut on a tablesaw. Instead, use your circular saw and a straight-edge guide, like the one described in "Skill Builder: Making an Edge Guard" on p. 79. When sanding, it's easy to accidentally round over an edge or end. To correct this, cut a small amount off both sides and/or ends

A

Simple scraping system. Draw pencil lines across the top to make sure the entire surface gets attention. Unlike planes, scrapers don't need to go with the grain. Working diagonally quickly levels ridges between boards.

rather than simply making two cuts to final dimension. Use a block plane or larger bench plane to remove any blade marks from the sides or ends (see photo B).

4. Hard maple holds an edge sharp enough to slice skin. Use a chamfer bit to rout a ⅛"-deep chamfer on the top edge and a ³/₁₆"-deep chamfer on the bottom edge. To avoid burning, take light passes and don't stop moving the router midcut.

B

Cutting the top down to size. **Trimming a large tabletop can be tricky—even on a full-size table-saw. Use your circular saw and edge guide to size the panel.**

Building the Base

The leg and apron assembly must be strong enough to resist the racking pressure exerted on the legs every time it's pushed across a floor. In this case, mortise and tenon joinery is the best choice—the large tenons provide mechanical strength and plenty of surface area for glue. To cut the eight identical tenons (two for each leg), you'll use a shopmade mortising template.

Cutting and milling the aprons

1. The back apron and back rail start as one wider board. Start with a board that's at least 5½" wide and crosscut it to 46". Measure in 3" from both ends to establish the outside edges of the ¾"-wide side dadoes (used to house the side dividers). The center dado should be in the dead center of the board—find the center of the back apron and measure ⅜" to either side of the line.

2. To rout the three dadoes, use the alternate side of your edge guide. Set your router to make a ¼"-deep cut and make the first pass. Reposition the guide to complete the ¾"-wide dado. Use the dado cut on the T-end as a guide to locate the bit. Repeat the sequence to rout the remaining two dadoes, as shown in photo C.

C

Double up the dadoes. **Making the back apron and lower rail from the same board ensures that the dadoes line up when the back rail assembly is glued together.**

3. After routing the dadoes, rip a ¾" strip from one edge of your back apron stock. Next, set your tablesaw fence to 4½" and rip the back apron to final width. While you're at it, rip the boards you plan to use to make the side aprons, stub aprons, and false drawer fronts.

4. After cutting the apron stock to width, crosscut the side aprons 21½". To make the front stub aprons easier to hold and position when mortising, leave them 2" to 3" long, then trim them to length after mortising.

5. The next step is to mortise the aprons in order to attach them to the legs. Use your router and a mortise guide to rout a ⁵/₁₆" by 3¼" by 1⅛"-deep mortise centered on the ends of all the apron pieces, as shown in "Skill Builder: Simple Slot Mortiser" and photo D on p. 160.

6. You can also use the jig to mortise the legs. Reposition the hardwood fence to cut a mortise centered ⁷/₁₆" in from the outside edge of the leg. This layout should leave a very small reveal (about ¹/₁₆") where the leg meets the apron. The reveal is easier to deal with than a flush apron-to-leg joint, but small enough so that you don't have to worry about sanding.

7. After routing the mortises, cut the stock for the loose tenons. Since you've made the mortising jig, take the time to make extra tenon stock for later projects. If you own a planer, planing scrap stock to make the ⁵/₁₆"-wide tenons is a simple task. If you don't, you can use your tablesaw. Resaw your loose tenon stock as close as you can to final dimension, then build a planing sled as shown in photo E. Tack a pair of ⁵/₁₆" strips to the scrapwood sled to give your plane rails to ride on. Plane down the tenon stock until it's even with the strips. You'll find that rounding over the edges of loose tenons is a lot easier than trying to square off the ends of your mortises (see photo F).

D

Mortising made simple. The template makes mortising easier, but not foolproof. Make sure that the apron is securely clamped to your bench and the jig is clamped to the wood before routing.

E

Perfect planing sled. Rest the sole of your plane against the ⁵/₁₆"-thick guides and plane down the tenon strip to width. Stop planing as soon as you start shaving off the pencil marks on the strips.

F

Rounding the corners. Rounding over the edges of the tenon stock on a router table is easier than squaring the ends of the router-cut mortises with a chisel. Alternately, you can use a file.

G

Template-guided buttonholer. Using a ½"-diameter guide bushing and this two-piece jig, you can quickly rout mortises sized to fit hardwood tabletop fasteners.

8. Hardwood buttons secure the base to the top, but unlike in earlier chapters (refer to "Skill Builder: Making Tabletop Fasteners" on p. 115, you'll rout individual mortises, or buttonholes, instead of grooving the top of each

JIG: BUTTON-SLOT JIG

This jig makes routing a shallow mortise for a hardwood tabletop fastener as quick and easy as cutting a slot with your biscuit jointer. Cut a small piece of ⅜"-thick acrylic as shown, then attach it to a wood fence so that the cutout is centered ⅜" down from the edge of the board.

Outfit your router with a ¼"-diameter straight or spiral bit and a ½" O.D. bushing. Set the plunge depth to ⅜", then bore both ends to full depth. Remove the waste between the holes with two or three progressively deeper passes.

BUTTONHOLE MORTISES

Use this router jig with a ¼"-diameter spiral bit and ½" O.D. bushing to rout the ⅜"-wide by 1¼"-long mortise. Set the depth stop to rout a ⅜"-deep mortise.

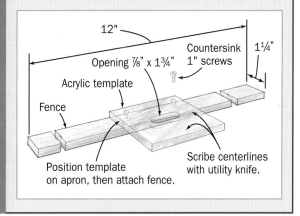

12"
Opening ⅞" x 1¾"
Countersink 1" screws
1¼"
Acrylic template
Fence
Position template on apron, then attach fence.
Scribe centerlines with utility knife.

apron. Compared to the groove you cut for the earlier projects, the smaller mortises are less likely to cause the top edge to split. (Buttonholes can also be routed after assembly, a useful trick should you forget a step in the future.)

Build the jig shown above, then make a few test mortises on a piece of scrap to make sure the top edge of your buttons are flush with the apron's top edge (see photo G).

What You'll Need

- ■ **Router**
- ■ **¼"-diameter straight bit or spiral upcut bit**
- ■ **⁷/₁₆" O.D. bushing**
- ■ **⅜"-thick acrylic**
- ■ **12" combination square**
- ■ **Hardwood strips**
- ■ **½"-diameter Forstner bit**
- ■ **File**
- ■ **1" wood screws**
- ■ **⅛"-diameter drill bit**
- ■ **Countersink bit**
- ■ **Drill**

For a large number of mortises, you can save time by using a routing template, such as the one shown on the facing page. The template and bushing work together to guide the bit.

By using different combinations of bushings and bits, you can change the offset, or distance between the bit and template, to create different-size mortises. For example, using this template with a ¼" bit and ⁷/₁₆" O.D. bushing will create a mortise that's ⁵/₁₆" wide by 3¼" long. Using a ½" O.D. bushing restricts the movement so that the bit cuts a mortise just ¼" by 3", a mortise suitably sized for smaller tables.

The legs come premortised, so we'll focus attention on the aprons. But you can also use this jig to mortise shopmade legs. Simply lay out the mortise location, then install new fences to reposition the template.

Better than a pencil. Use a razor knife to scribe lines to mark out the mortise. They're a surer guide than those marked out with a pencil.

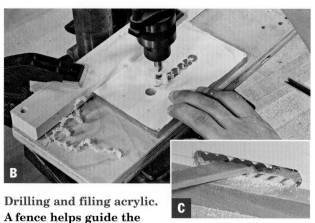

Drilling and filing acrylic. A fence helps guide the drill bit and prevents the piece from spinning should the bit freeze in the hole. File down the ridges to make a smooth slot.

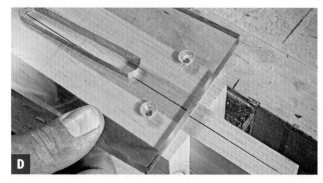

Setting the template. To position the template, clamp a scrap piece of apron stock between the guides. Look at the scribed line directly overhead to ensure that it's correctly positioned.

Simple Slot Mortiser

To mill exact mortises, use this router jig with a ¼"-diameter spiral bit and ⁷⁄₁₆" O.D. bushing to mill a ⁵⁄₁₆"-wide mortise. You may also use a ½" O.D. bushing to rout a ¼"-wide mortise.

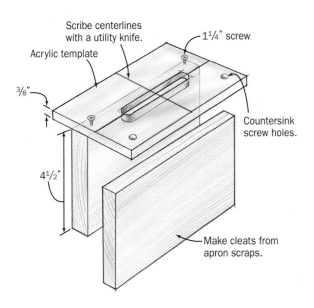

Scribe centerlines with a utility knife.

1¼" screw

Acrylic template

³⁄₈"

Countersink screw holes.

4½"

Make cleats from apron scraps.

1. Cut a template blank from a piece of ³⁄₈" acrylic. (Plywood also works, but the clear acrylic makes it easier to position on your stock.) Lay out the centerlines on the blank, then incise those lines with a utility knife (see photo A). Next, lay out a 3½" by ½" mortise, centered on the crosshairs.

2. Use a ½"-diameter Forstner bit to drill out the mortise slot (see photo B). To prevent burning the acrylic and fusing the plastic to the bit, use a slow drill speed and an in-and-out action so the plastic has a chance to cool.

After drilling a series of holes, clamp the template in your bench vise and file away the remaining crescents (see photo C). File carefully, but realize that a few minor divots won't

really matter—the bushing will ride over small dips without affecting the fit of the joint.

3. Use a combination square to mark the center of the stock you're mortising. Clamp your centering board and two additional short pieces in your bench vise (see photo D). Clamp the template to the three boards as you drill pilot holes, countersink, and then drive four 1¼" screws to permanently attach the template to the cleats.

4. Draw a centerline on a test piece of apron and clamp it in the bench vise. Place the guide on top, align the shorter scribe line with the marks on the apron, and clamp in place. Use the jig to plunge-cut both ends of the mortise, then rout out the waste between the ends of the mortise in a series of shallower (⅛" to ¼") passes, as shown in the in photo D on p. 158.

One problem you may encounter when routing mortises is chip buildup. Periodically lift the router off the jig and brush or vacuum out the mortise (see photo E).

Making the plunge. Set the depth adjustment, then plunge-cut both ends of your mortise. Make ⅛"-deep passes to connect the holes. Vacuum out sawdust before the buildup damages the bit or bushing.

Assembling the base

1. Before assembling the base, rip two ¾" by ½" by 46" strips to make the front rails. Next, cut two 4"-long by 3"-wide spacer blocks and glue them between the front rails (see photo A). The two side dividers will fit into the dadoes in the back rail and against the ends of the spacer blocks on the front rail assembly. The center divider does not have a spacer block to reference against, but it will provide additional reinforcement to the rails once it's glued and screwed in place (see photo H).

2. Glue the back bottom rail to the bottom edge of the back apron. Make sure the dadoes don't slide out of alignment as you tighten the clamps. The center and side dividers should be able to slide down and into the waiting dadoes.

3. You're now ready to turn these parts into a desk. Assemble the sides first. Apply a light swipe of glue to the loose tenons, then slip them into the mortises in the side aprons. Then slide the tenons into the leg mortises (see photo I).

Try to work quickly; because the tenons are designed to fit tightly, there's a chance that the wood might start to swell, or the glue

Back rail guides front frame glue-up. In order for the dividers to fit squarely in the base, the spacer blocks on the front rail must line up with the outside edges of the dadoes in the back apron.

Assemble the side aprons first. Assembling the sides upside down on your workbench or assembly table ensures that the top edge of the side aprons stays flush with the top ends of the legs.

Clamping and squaring the base. After clamping up the back apron, measure across the diagonals to see if the base is square. If not, clamp diagonally to make the corner-to-corner measurements equal.

Screw the rail assembly to the stub aprons. Drill and countersink the holes in the back of the front rail assembly, then fasten it to the stub aprons with 1¼" screws.

might grab, which would prevent the ends of the aprons from tightly abutting against the legs. If that happens, try tapping the legs with a rubber mallet or applying extra elbow grease to the panel clamp (see photo I).

4. Cut the stub aprons to length and install them to the front legs. Use your combination square to ensure that they remain perpendicular to the legs as you tighten the clamps.

5. To attach the back apron, set both side assemblies on your bench, bottom up. Apply

glue to the loose tenons, then slide them into the mortises in the back apron. The clamping pressure should be enough to pull the legs against the ends of the back apron. Position the front rail behind the stub tenons to square up the base. To ensure that the top will sit flat against the aprons, clamp all three aprons to the top of the bench (see photo J).

6. Once the glue has dried, attach the front rail assembly to the stub aprons using 1¼"-long wood screws (see photo K).

Installing the drawer guides

Each guide consists of three parts: the divider (two side and one center), the bottom runner that supports the drawer from underneath, and the top kicker that keeps the drawer from tipping downward when the drawer is opened. By carefully fitting the kickers and runners between the front rail assembly and back apron, you'll also add rigidity to the base.

1. Start by cutting the dividers to width. Use the materials list on p. 154 as a guide, but note that they must fit between the front rails and sit flush with the front face of the rail assembly.

2. Make the kickers and runners next. Again, refer to the dimensions given in the materials list, but double-check the length

Attaching the kickers. Attach kickers to the top of each divider with 1¼" screws. Cut the strips so that they fit tightly between the back apron and front rails.

Double-check the center divider. The center divider must be square with the front rails. Position carefully, then attach the center divider to front rails with 1¼" screws.

against your actual project. You don't need a planer to make the ½"-thick strips. Cut the pieces to rough dimensions, then resaw them to width on your tablesaw. Attach the strips to the to the dividers with 1½" screws (see photo L on p. 164), then handplane (if necessary) so that they are flush with the top and bottom edges of the front and back aprons (see photo L). (Note that the left and right drawer guides are mirror images of each other. The side runners and kickers should protrude into the drawer opening.)

3. Attach the side and center dividers to the front rails with 1¼" screws. Make sure that the center divider is centered on the front rail (the drawer openings on either side should be the same size) before screwing it in place (see photo M).

4. You're now ready to permanently attach the drawer guides to the base. Remove the runners and kickers. Next, apply glue to the back end of the dividers, then slide the dividers back into the dadoes in the back apron. Reattach the kickers and runners to the dividers with glue and screws.

5. Unlike the back apron, the front rail isn't thick enough to hold hardwood buttons. Instead, you'll secure the front of the top by driving a 1"-long screw through the center kicker. Drill and countersink a ⅛"-diameter hole through the center of the middle kicker. (You do not need to enlarge this hole. Regardless of how much the top expands and contracts, it should remain centered on the base.

Making and Fitting the Drawer

The drawer sides attach to the front and back using a locking rabbet joint (see the drawing at right). Unlike the simple dadoed drawers used in the earlier projects, the interlocking parts used here produce a stronger joint, without the need for additional pins or nails. This is important when you consider how often these drawers will be opened and closed over the desk's lifetime. The joint also enables you to install the back of the drawer at the very back end of the sides. The false back and long plywood bottom creates a "secret" compartment that won't be visible unless you pull the drawer completely out of the base.

This joint isn't that difficult to make. It involves cutting a dado along the inside face of the sides to fit onto a tongue cut on the front and back. You'll use your tablesaw and flat-toothed blade (such as one of the outside blades from your dado cutter) to cut the front and back, and your router, router table, and ⅛"-diameter straight bit to dado the sides. Using two machines will enable you to carefully set each to cut half the joint and keep those settings until you finish cutting all the needed pieces.

1. Using the drawer openings as your guide, rip the ½"-thick drawer stock so that it slides easily into the drawer cavity. Next, crosscut four pieces ⅛" shorter than the width of the opening to make the two fronts and backs. Finally, crosscut four side pieces to length.

2. To make the joint, start by slotting the ends of the fronts and backs. Beginning with one of the fronts, adjust the height of the bit to the thickness of your drawer sides, in this

Locking Rabbets on the Drawers

Cutting the front and back on your tablesaw and the sides with your router is more efficient than using one tool because you can save your settings once you achieve a tight-fitting joint.

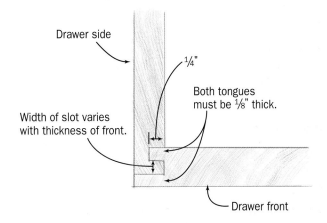

Drawer side

¼"

Both tongues must be ⅛" thick.

Width of slot varies with thickness of front.

Drawer front

case ½". Next, adjust your fence so that the blade will cut a slot roughly in the center of the board. Make a test cut, then flip the stock and make a second pass (see photo A on p. 166). (This is the same technique you used to make a centered groove in the sofa table rails.) Next, measure the width of the tongues. Adjust the fence as necessary to produce two tongues that are exactly ⅛" thick. Once set, slot the ends of the remaining front and backs.

Instead of struggling to measure the width of the test tongues, you can create a test board by routing a ⅛" groove on a piece of scrap. Aim for a snug, not tight, fit that goes together with only slight hand pressure. If it's too tight, you may wind up breaking the joint during assembly.

3. The next step is to trim back the inside tongue to fit into the dadoed sides. Lower the blade to about ³⁄₁₆" high, then adjust the fence to cut a ¼"-long tongue. (To prevent the small cutoff from getting stuck between the blade and fence, clamp a spacer block against the fence as shown in photo B.) Using your miter gauge, cut the inside tongue on the front and back pieces.

4. After cutting the fronts and backs on your tablesaw, use your router table to dado the sides. Set the height of the bit to ¼", then attach a fence so that the dado starts ¼" in from the end of the board. Cut a test dado and see how well it fits with a front or back piece (see photo C). You may need to tweak the height of the bit or position of the fence before dadoing the sides.

5. After cutting the locking rabbet, the rest of the joinery is a piece of cake. Using your router table or dado cutter, cut a ¼"-deep groove along the inside faces of the drawer pieces for the bottoms. Next, cut a ½"-wide by ¼"-deep dado 4½" from the back ends of the

Slotting the front and back. To make the centered slot on the front and back pieces of the drawer, flip the stock so that both faces are running against the fence. Adjust the width of the slot so that both tongues are ⅛" thick.

Cut down the inside tongue. Trim the tongues on the inside faces of the drawer front and back to fit the dadoes in the drawer sides. Clamp a spacer block against the fence so that the cutoff doesn't get trapped between the blade and fence.

Use test stock to find a fit. Adjust the height of the bit, then the location of the fence, until the front and back attach to the sides like a lock and key. Be careful not to break off a tongue when test-fitting.

sides for the false back. Assemble a drawer without glue and double-check the measurements for the plywood bottom before cutting the bottom to size.

6. You're now ready to assemble the drawers. Apply glue to the locking rabbets on the front and back pieces and press them onto one side. Next, wipe a small amount of glue into the bottom groove, then slide in the plywood. Finally, install the false back (see photo D).

The plywood bottom should automatically square up the drawer, but measure the distance between opposite corners or use a plywood triangle (see "Jig: Squaring Triangles" on p. 67) to be sure. If the drawer is out of square, it won't fit into the opening.

Installing the false back. Apply a dab of glue to the dadoes in the drawer sides, then slide in the false back. The rear compartment isn't visible unless the drawer is removed from the desk.

Applying a Two-Part Finish

The desk makes use of two different finishes: I painted the base with pitch-black milk paint and used a wiping varnish to seal and protect the top.

Refer to p. 26 for a list of the basic ingredients you'll need to make a homemade wipe-on varnish.

Finishing the base

The dark paint ties the base together by hiding mineral streaks (common in soft maple) and also directs attention to the top. Using milk paint is also an effective way to camouflage future dents and dinks. For more information about mixing and applying milk paint, refer to p. 52.

1. Hand-sand the legs and aprons to 220-grit. Wipe down the surfaces with a damp rag, then lightly scuff-sand with 220-or 320-grit to remove any whiskers. Apply at

> **WORK SMART**
>
> To create an instant "antique" piece, consider layering two or more colors of milk paint. The top coat will hide the colors underneath, but burnishing the corners and edges will reveal the earlier layers to mimic a piece that's survived multiple generations. For burnishing, use 000 steel wool.

least two coats of milk paint to the legs and aprons, as shown in photo A, allowing a day for the paint to dry between coats.

2. When the second coat has dried, rub down the surface of the paint with a maroon abrasive pad. As soon as the paint begins to look a little shiny, switch over to 000 steel wool and continue burnishing. When the surface achieves a uniform gloss, wipe on a coat of wiping varnish or boiled linseed oil.

A

Painting ties it all together. Milk paint is a perfect way to conceal mineral streaks and future dents. The fine-grained hardwood needs only two coats before burnishing and applying oil.

Finishing the top

Using aniline dyes is a good way to accentuate the grain in the top. Unlike pigment-type stains that concentrate in the areas of the wood that have large pores (like end grain) or lie on top, dyes penetrate into the wood fibers, increasing the depth and contrast of the wood. Dyes come in powdered form; they can be mixed full strength or watered down to produce a lighter hue. Try finishing a test board until you're happy with the color.

1. Like milk paint, water-soluble dye stains will raise the grain of the wood. Before staining, wipe down the top and bottom of your desk with a damp rag, let it dry, then knock off the whiskers by lightly hand-sanding (with the grain) using 220-grit or 320-grit sandpaper.

2. Mix up your stain using the directions that come with the dye—the rule of thumb is to dissolve approximately 1 ounce of dye into

B

Just add water. Water-soluble aniline dye adds color without hiding the grain. Add the powder gradually to warm water while stirring.

C

Keep a wet edge. Dye stains aren't likely to leave streaks, provided that you work fairly quickly. For more color, apply more stain after the first coat has dried.

2 quarts of very hot (but not boiling) water (see photo B on p. 166). Using less powder than what's recommended will produce a lighter dye; if you use more, it will settle to the bottom of the jar.

3. To apply the stain, simply wipe it on with a rag or wide foam brush, as shown in photo C. To avoid stripes, or lap marks, coat the entire surface before it has time to dry. Once coated, you can wipe off excess with a rag or wait for the top to dry. Should the stain raise the grain, buff the surface with a white abrasive

pad or 320-grit sandpaper. Be careful not to sand to hard, or you might create a light-colored patch on your top.

4. Allow the top a full day to dry before applying any finish. Apply a generous first coat of wipe-on varnish, then wipe off the excess when it begins to feel tacky. Continue the application process for two or three days, then allow the top an extra two or three days to cure before applying a wax top coat.

Final Assembly

You're almost done. Now that the base, top, and drawers are done, all that's left is to pull everything together.

1. It's easier to install the false drawer fronts before attaching the top. Install the drawers and position the false fronts so that the gaps between the stub aprons and false fronts are as even as possible. Temporarily secure the false fronts with clamps, then screw them in place (see photo A).

2. Remove the drawers from the base, then lay a blanket on your bench and place the top face down. Center the upside-down base over the top (see photo B). Drill ⅛"-diameter pilot holes to install the button fasteners. When you attach the buttons, back off the screws by ¼-turn to allow a little wiggle room. Drill one pilot hole through the center divider and install a 1¼" screw to lock the top to the base. After that, sit back and admire your handwork.

A

Fitting the false fronts. Adjust the fronts so that the gaps along both ends are even and the top edge is slightly below the top edge of the stub aprons.

B

Buttoning down the top. Center the base on the top and drill pilot holes to attach the hardwood fasteners. Use a hardwood stop block to ensure that you don't drill through the top.

Sources

BOSCH POWER TOOLS
1800 W. Central Rd.
Mt. Prospect, IL 60056
877-267-2499
www.boschtools.com
Handheld and benchtop power tools.

CLASSIC DESIGNS BY MATTHEW BURAK
P.O. Box 329
84 Central St.
St Johnsbury, VT 05819
802-748-9378 or 800-843-7405
www.classicdesigns.com
Maker of the legs used in the desk project.

FRANKLIN INTERNATIONAL
2020 Bruck St.
Columbus, Ohio 43207
800-877-4583
www.franklininternational.com
Maker of many different adhesives to match all sorts of woodworking and construction projects.

FREUD AMERICA, INC.
218 Feld Ave.
High Point, NC 27263
800-334-4107, 800-263-7016
www.freudtools.com
For the blades and bits used throughout this book.

LEE VALLEY TOOLS
P.O. Box 1780
Ogdensburg, NY 13669-6780
800-871-8158, 800-267-8735
www.leevalley.com
Mail-order source for all sorts of power and hand tools, as well as supplies.

LIE-NIELSEN TOOLWORKS, INC.
P.O. Box 9
Warren, ME 04864-0009
800-327-2520
www.lie-nielsen.com
High-end hand tools.

THE OLD FASHIONED MILK PAINT CO., INC.
436 Main St.
Groton, MA 01450
866-350-6455
www.milkpaint.com
Maker of the milk paint used in the blanket box and desk projects.

PORTER CABLE/DELTA
4825 Hwy. 45 N.
Jackson, TN 38302-2468
800-487-8665
www.porter-cable.com
www.deltamachinery.com
Makers of almost every type of stationary, benchtop, and handheld power tool.

ROCKLER WOODWORKING AND HARDWARE
4365 Willow Dr.
Medina, MN 55340
800-279-4441
www.rockler.com
Mail-order source for tools, hardware, and finishes.

TWIN OAKS LUMBER LLC
(supplier of material used to build the projects in this book)
2345 Sinsinawa Rd.
Hazel Green, WI 53818
608-748-4803
A fine local source of domestic and exotic hardwoods and softwoods.

WOODCRAFT SUPPLY CORP.
1177 Rosemar Rd.
P.O. Box 1686
Parkersburg, WV 26102
800-225-1153
www.woodcraft.com
Mail-order source for ¼"- and ½"-thick exotic and domestic hardwoods, as well as other woodworking tools and materials.

Index

Note: page references in italics indicate a photograph; references in bold indicate an illustration.